WORK, ETHICS &
ORGANISATIONAL LIFE

2ND EDITION

JOHN G. CULLEN

Published by OAK TREE PRESS
Cork, Ireland
www.oaktreepress.com / www.SuccessStore.com

© 2018 John Cullen

A catalogue record of this book is available from the British Library.

ISBN 978 1 78119 336 5 (paperback)
ISBN 978 1 78119 337 2 (ePub)
ISBN 978 1 78119 338 9 (Kindle)
ISBN 978 1 78119 339 6 (PDF)

Cover design: Kieran O'Connor.
Cover image: © Martin Bech / 123rf.com

CONTENTS

ACKNOWLEDGEMENTS & DEDICATION

This second edition of *Work, Ethics & Organisational Life* is primarily a response to the questions of my undergraduate and postgraduate students at Maynooth University School of Business, whose engagement with these concepts in class has shaped the way in which the ideas are presented in this work. The field of *business & society* is constantly evolving and, as new geo-political, social and environmental issues arise, it is important to address the impact these new developments have on theory and corporate practice, in a prompt fashion. Brian O'Kane of Oak Tree Press has always been a hugely understanding and supportive publisher, and I'm very grateful for the support that he has given to each edition of this ongoing writing project.

I graduated from Maynooth University almost quarter of a century ago, and it is striking to still see the enormous regard that students and staff still have for this very special institution of higher education. My colleagues at Maynooth University, primarily in the School of Business, but also in every other faculty, could not be more supportive in encouraging intellectual exploration. University academics should not only support each other in research, teaching and writing, but also in our societal and service roles. As I hope to communicate in this book, *organisational life* is much more than turning up for work, getting paid and leaving. I feel privileged to have experienced deep professional friendship from all my colleagues in Maynooth University.

Professional support does not only come from work colleagues. Many valued friends, family members, my 'in-laws', as well as colleagues outside the university have made a huge difference to how I think about work and the value that it can create. My parents could never have encouraged me more to pursue my vocation as an academic and I'll always be grateful to them for the opportunities they provided me. My wife and our children have always been hugely supportive of my teaching, research and writing and I thank them for their love and patience.

This edition of *Work, Ethics & Organisational Life* is dedicated to my son, Adam.

1: Introducing Work, Ethics & Organisational Life

This book introduces the topic of business ethics to readers who have not read anything about it before. It aims to present the foundations of ethical theory to people who must study it as part of a course, or to people who might be curious about the moral foundations of how we work, manage and make money in contemporary late capitalist society. In short, it is a book for people who are *learning* about ethics for the first time.

Although *Work, Ethics & Organisational Life* has been written for first-time students of ethics, it does not presuppose that its readers have never reflected on the nature of morality. Nor does it imagine that its readers have never 'done' ethics before. In fact, the opposite is the case: *Work, Ethics & Organisational Life* is written from the perspective that the vast majority of our decisions, behaviours and cultural norms are deeply inscribed and influenced by moral frameworks, although often we simply don't have the time to recognise this.

Contemporary life is full of choice – and all choices are, at heart, ethical decisions that have consequences for the individuals who make them, and the groups, societies and organisations that are impacted by them. We often simply do not think about the implications of the decisions that we make. More importantly, we often fail to consider that the decisions we make have been scripted by cultural norms, organisational strategies and societal expectations of us.

Ethical theory allows us to look under the surface of these silent, unobserved, yet influential forces that exert a huge influence on how we think and how we live our lives. Ethical theory can help us understand ourselves, who we are, what we are *for* and how we can change our world.

Most business ethics textbooks have titles that reflect their intention to discuss business-related moral theories only. But, if we fail to consider ethics as a broader, interdisciplinary field informed by philosophy, sociology, cultural studies, critical theory and psychoanalysis, as well as more 'mainstream' fields of business studies, such as organisational behaviour, economics, strategy and marketing, we run the risk of presenting business ethics as a dry, overly-theoretical field abstracted from how people actually work and manage in their everyday lives.

'Work', 'ethics' and 'organisational life' are the three key concerns of this text, but it is important from the outset to demonstrate the extent to which these areas are not only inter-related, but are actually informed by each other in the very way that they are constituted.

WORK

Work is often presented as one of the necessary evils of modern life. We work to earn the money needed to pay for the necessities of life and to engage in activities that we really want to do. Thinking about work solely in economic terms negates those ways in which we can consider it as a deeper indication of who we are as active citizens and as intellectual, ethical and spiritual beings. Dictionary definitions of work usually define it along of the lines of 'the application of organised physical and/or mental energy to achieve a goal'. Work, however, is much more than tasks and responsibilities from which we, or other people, derive economic value (such as payment, or returns on our investments). It actually involves much more than this, and as we will see in **Chapter 3**, the *ethics* of how people choose to work has long been regarded as one of the most important factors in the success of commercial ventures. Work, however, also exists outside formal organised contexts, and we are actually at work in many more ways than we are actually aware of. Psychoanalysis, for example, has demonstrated that our psyche is actually a very 'busy' place, where conscious and unconscious elements of our minds demand energy and often compete and conflict with each other. Psychoanalysis can provide a very important perspective that assists us in understanding how our ethical orientations impact our daily working lives, and how our unconscious minds in turn contribute to ethical structures at political, social and organisational levels. Psychoanalysis, as a method for understanding business, ethics and society, is an important framework for this book and it will be discussed in more detail later in this chapter.

ETHICS

Ethics can be an inherently difficult subject to learn, because although there are a number of pre-existing discourses on what it is as a subject, we often experience and 'do' ethics at a very subjective level. Ethics is derived from the Greek word *ethos*, meaning 'custom', which is why ethics is often described as code or set of principles by which groups of people actually (or should) live. Most of the social sciences are, arguably, concerned with understanding how we unconsciously act as individuals, groups and members of organisations or societies. Ethics is different to studies of organisational sociology and organisational behaviour, which are concerned with the way things are, or how they can be changed or managed. The study of ethics is concerned with developing in students a level of critical reflexivity that assists them to question taken-for-granted assumptions about the world.

Educators often say that they require their students to demonstrate 'critical thinking' or 'reflexivity' in their work, but what exactly does this mean? The management academic Ann Cunliffe identified (2004) three levels of reflexivity:

o **Reflex interaction:** Where individuals do not think about their actions and react to social 'cues' in an unconscious manner;

o **Reflective analysis:** Where individuals think about what they have encountered in their working life and try to learn from it;

o **Critical reflexivity:** Where individuals consider their attempts to learn about themselves in the workplace in the context of broader social discourses, *asking why* the social world is constructed the way it is in the first place.

Elliot Aronson (2004) wrote that people are motivated to justify their actions, beliefs and feelings and, when they do something, they attempt to convince themselves that they acted rationality and ethically. We need to do this to reduce our cognitive dissonance (Festinger, 1957), which is a state of tension that results when we simultaneously 'hold' inconsistent beliefs about the same thing. Cognitive dissonance is unpleasant to experience and individuals are compelled to reduce it, often by compromising one set of cognitions *versus* another. One way in which this is done is through justifying their actions or decisions after they have taken them, by finding or interpreting information that upholds their views or beliefs – for example, following a difficult decision in a scenario that lacked a clear, positive outcome.

From an ethical perspective, it is important to be conscious of the role of self-justification in our ethical behaviour. Violent behaviour towards, and mistreatment of, humans and animals is often self-justified by perpetrators' beliefs that their victims somehow 'deserved' what happened to them.

Aronson's work as a social psychologist underpins many of the day-to-day ways in which people self-justify their behaviour. The concept of justification is useful to studying ethics as it demonstrates how we participate in, and perpetuate, larger ethical discourses through supporting or resisting decisions that others take. To understand this, we must address one of the most important issues that everyone must face: our own mortality.

The psychoanalyst and cultural theorist Julia Kristeva claims that contemporary secular discourse and philosophy cannot successfully accommodate the inevitability of death, which has meant that secularism is in crisis and religious/spiritual traditions are not (2012). In other words, if you have a religious faith, the issue of death is 'sorted' and you do not have to worry about having a finite existence; if you do not have a religious faith, the fact of death means that you have a limited amount of time to live. Some people accept this, but some philosophers have explored what this fact 'does' to people who don't see this life as a step to the next world. In the 16th century, the French philosopher Michel de Montaigne identified humanity's mortal nature as the driver for ethical, philosophical and sociological thinking about the meaning of existence. In a famous essay, 'To philosophise is to learn how to die', de Montaigne wrote:

> We do not know where death awaits us: so let us wait for it everywhere. To practice death is to practice freedom. A man who has learned how to die has unlearned how to be a slave. Knowing how to die gives us freedom from subjection and constraint. (2003: 96)

De Montaigne could probably afford to be optimistic about death, given that he was a devout Christian. In *The Denial of Death* (2011), Ernest Becker wrote that all human beings sooner or later must engage with the most difficult fact of their existence: the fact that they will die. People do this by becoming involved in an 'immortality project', which is a way of reminding ourselves that our existence is significant. The social construction of these projects leads to conflicts between these systems over time. The people who organise, run and participate in the activities or terrorist or racist groups ultimately believe that they are doing the right thing for themselves, their community, and even the world. Even if this involves inflicting injustice on other people, they believe that they are being just. Becker proposed that people become mentally ill and depressed because they are denied access to resources that could enable them to complete their immortality project. Boring work, poverty and lack of opportunity become sources of deep dissatisfaction. Ethics can literally become a matter of life-or-death.

One of the most detailed (and complex) discussions of justification was provided by Luc Boltanski and Laurent Thévenot in *On Justification* (2006), a scholarly examination of the sources of justification as they have emerged over the centuries of Europe's transformation from feudal aristocracies and monarchies to industrialisation. The text's erudition makes it seem impenetrable to readers at times, but as a work of cultural sociology it offers some very useful frameworks for examining the different ways in which certain positions (or logics) value types of ethical actions in various fashions. To greatly oversimplify this work, Boltanski & Thévenot propose that there are six main logics (or 'polities') by which action is justified in ethical terms.

The first of these is the logic of the *market*, which ascribes worth to the goods that are produced and consumed in economic systems. In other words, people who follow this rationale believe that organising societies in a way that privileges market competition will result in all members benefitting when one member succeeds.

The second logic Boltanski & Thévenot name as *inspiration*. This perspective is very much based on the dominant religious and spiritual dimensions that, for many people, provide their ethical framework. The concept of God's grace dominates this perspective, which essentially emphasises self-denial and humility. The *inspiration* perspective advocates making ethical decisions on the basis of charity and compassion, rather than individualistic achievement. It should be pointed out that, although the ethical logic of inspiration emerges from a particular religious framework, Boltanski & Thévenot do not insist that religious faith is required to participate in it. However, the religious roots of this orientation mean that people who are inspired by it do not require the esteem of other people to benefit from it. Rather, a lack of concern for one's personal interests in favour of other people is the foundation of the logic of inspiration.

Inspiration is the opposite of the logic of *fame*, which values worth on the basis of the opinion of others. According to this opposing logic, the more people who are aware of an individual and value their importance, the more worth that person has. It must be pointed out that this has nothing to do with an individual's self-esteem but rather pertains to the number of people who value an individual as the determinant of the individual's worth. This may appear to be a very superficial and narcissistic way of valuing people, but it is worth bearing in mind that it stems from the work of the highly influential 17th century philosopher Thomas Hobbes, and can be used to analyse contemporary social problems in a consumer-oriented society. For example, the sociologist Zygmunt Bauman (1998, 2011) has long warned against the way in which contemporary society has a created an ethic of consumption. In this consumer society, a person is valued on their ability to consume whatever they choose from the market. The poorer a person is, the less they will be able to choose what they can consume and this will result in them feeling depressed or marginalised. When individuals are pushed to the margins of any group, they become dangerous either to themselves or the group.

The consumer society, however, does not only value those who can consume; it also values people who can *be* consumed by the market. This means that people who have attained celebrity, or uncommon skill sets, are also more valued in society in general. This ethic of consumption is dangerous in that it has the potential to marginalise groups of people. During the London riots in summer 2011, groups of primarily young men who were unemployed or underemployed (and thus did not have the economic power to fully participate in the consumer society, and who were not themselves *consumed* by the labour market) engaged in criminal activity and violence. Although these riots originally stemmed from a protest against a police shooting of a black man, they soon descended into wide-scale looting and civil disorder. It is interesting to note that the main targets of the riots (which soon spread across the UK) were centres of consumption (shopping centres and department stores). To claim that the riots were the result of people being denied opportunities for *fame* is to oversimplify, but the London riots demonstrate the extent to which it has become a powerful influence in society.

The next logic is one based on classical considerations of how society should be organised in a hierarchy, and the places that individuals occupy in this hierarchy. This *domestic* logic might be construed as an ethics of care (where individuals should be concerned with the concrete wellbeing of those they are closest to).

Similar to this *domestic* logic is the *civic logic*, where individuals should think of their worth as citizens serving the general interest or the common good. Rather than subordinating themselves to a network of individual relationships (as in the *domestic* logic), they should instead focus on what is best for people, because people don't always act in ways that serve the general good.

The final logic (the *industrial* logic) takes the *civil* logic one step further. It proposes that scientific principles should be applied to how society and social relations should be organised. Thus, utility is the highest organising principle and the satisfaction of social needs is paramount. The *industrial* logic proposes that social systems (such as nation-states) are best managed as if they were industrial factories, rather than cultures or social entities.

Justification of our actions is just one way in which we can think about how we unconsciously apply ethics to our everyday lives. It is, however, not the full story. One of the main points which ethicists and psychoanalysts share is that the work we do, and the organisations we do it in or for, are critical to us being our best ethical selves.

ORGANISATIONAL LIFE

Prior to the prologue of the 1971 classic horror novel, *The Exorcist*, author William Peter Blatty juxtaposes a quote from the Gospel of Mark with three shocking fragments of text:

o   The first is the transcript of a phone call between two Mafiosi delightfully recounting the extended torture of a victim;

o   The second is a quote from Tom Doorley's reaction to the maiming and slaughter of a priest and a group of boys by a platoon of Viet-Cong soldiers;

o   The third is simply a list of three death camps: Dachau, Auschwitz and Buchenwald.

Blatty is undoubtedly foregrounding his chilling tale of demonic possession (which was soon after transformed by William Friedkin into a modern cinematic masterpiece) by emphasising evil as a real and powerful force in the contemporary world. Nobody who disbelieves in the existence of the Devil doubts the existence of evil in the world!

What is interesting to me as a business academic interested in psychoanalytical approaches to studying people in organisations is that Blatty is describing acts of systematic cruelty that were conducted by people in an *organised context* as part of their *work*. Unfortunately, stories of barbarity, abuse and evil continue to permeate the world, but such acts are often more chilling when we consider that they are undertaken by organised groups of people who systematically plan and orchestrate them with what Norman Dixon called a 'mixture of brutality and bureaucracy' (1976: 275). It also asks the questions:

o What is it about the nature of working in organisations that makes people lose sight of their own ethical positions?

o Why do certain managers lose sight of the fact that remuneration is something to be earned rather than an entitlement?

o Why do certain organisations in specific sectors take risks in the full knowledge that, if they fail, other people will have to 'bail them out'?

o Casual workplace sexism, racism or discrimination is satirised in movies such as *Anchorman* or TV shows such as *The Office*, but what acts of discrimination do we unconsciously commit in our employment that would be unacceptable if we were to practice them in any other sphere of life?

o Why do some managers and executives make decisions that are not only pathological to individuals, communities and environmental locales, but even to their own organisations?

Occasionally the attempts of organisations to 'be ethical' or more socially responsible in their activities are lambasted as insincere attempts to fool customers and stakeholders into imagining that they are dealing with a business with a conscience. However, most organisations employ people who would like to make some positive difference to the world (or at least not cause unnecessary harm). Those who think that ethics should not be taught to business students and organisational managers often miss out on the huge benefits that businesses provide to society, and not just in terms of employment and economic growth.

This book attempts to examine business ethics in a way that relates directly to the real concerns of contemporary organisations by adopting a broadly psychoanalytic approach to examine the many issues at play in various workplaces that employees, managers and customers are often unaware of because they are obscured by accepted societal beliefs or cultural practices specific to certain sectors, occupations or organisations. Psychoanalytic theory has the potential to bring the frameworks, beliefs and values that we have hidden from ourselves into the light. As such, it is an incredibly relevant approach to understanding and applying ethics to the reality of day-to-day working and organisational life. Although readers may have a general sense of what psychoanalysis is and what it is for, some may wonder how it can be used to increase our understanding of workplaces and the relationship between business and society. This question will be addressed in the penultimate section of this chapter.

Engaging with the topic of ethics involves grappling with our taken-for-granted assumptions, particularly those we might not even be conscious of holding. These assumptions and beliefs, which we often believe are shared by everyone around us, impact on our behaviours and decisions in very significant ways. The ethical frameworks that we have inherited from our intellectual ancestors work on us at an intrinsic level.

Everyone responds to ethics as an academic discipline in a different way, and these responses in turn can tell us much about what type of ethical *personae* we hold as individuals. Learning about ethics, then, is very much about learning about the 'self' and the processes and functions that have constructed it. Our 'paradigms', or the limited ways in which we see the world, have been constructed over time for us by others. These paradigmatic worldviews shape not only *what* we think, but also *how* we think. 'Doing ethics' involves gaining an understanding of what these paradigmatic assumptions are, in order that we can change them so as to flourish as individuals. This questioning, however, is not easy, although students often demonstrate a remarkably broad range of understandings of what is meant by ethics.

Morality can be defined as the set of standards that an individual or a group holds in relation what is right and wrong, or good and evil. Moral standards manifest themselves as behavioural *norms* or *value* attached to certain objects or actions. These norms prime us to use certain prepared scripts when we are faced with moral dilemmas or uncertain situations.

A key element of learning ethics, particularly in the business context, is becoming aware of these scripts (which themselves emerge from larger societal discourses) so we can challenge them. The scripts that we use to tell ourselves that some things are ethical and others are not drive our implicitly-held ethical attitudes. These *implicit ethical attitudes* (introspectively unidentified or inaccurately identified traces of past experience that mediate favourable or unfavourable feeling, thought or action towards social objects) play a huge role in determining our behaviours, and perhaps more significantly, our decisions about important issues in our lives. If left unexamined, we run the risk of choosing careers, making business decisions and ultimately living lives that are devoid of real learning and of depriving ourselves of opportunities to flourish as full human beings, which is one of most important reasons why ethics is researched and studied.

Sometimes, when we respond to an ethical dilemma with an answer such as "it depends on the circumstances", it means that we are uncertain about expressing our ethical beliefs explicitly. It is not that we do not have moral standards, only that we are not entirely sure what they are. This is true for most people who do not always have an accessible moral code that they have inherited or decided to live by. We only become clear, then, about the nature of our implicit ethical attitudes when we are forced to exercise them in 'real-life' decisions about concrete dilemmas with significant consequences for our lives or the lives of others. Adopting an 'it depends' attitude is often misinterpreted as *ethical relativism*, which is the belief there are no universal moral standards that can be applied to all situations requiring a moral decision.

One way in which we can develop a clearer understanding of our implicit ethical attitudes is to examine our own process of moral reasoning by which we determine whether behaviours, institutions or policies accord with or violate our moral standards. Moral psychology often tries to unearth ethical attitudes through laboratory-type tests that aim to clarify the implicitly-held (Marquardt & Hoeger, 2009) or automatically-triggered (Reynolds *et al*, 2010) moral positions held by subjects.

Studying ethics affords us with an opportunity to look at this important area of our lives in more detail, with the aim of becoming aware of ourselves as ethical beings, so we can make enhanced ethical decisions in the future. Most people, and particularly managers, simply do not have the time to do this reflective work, and must make 'snap' decisions, often in pressurised contexts, and then deal with the personal and organisational consequences afterwards.

BUSINESS ETHICS

Business ethics is a specialised study of moral right and wrong that concentrates on moral standards as they apply to organisations, and behaviour in the context of organisational life. Business ethics only really began to be identified as an academic field in the 1980s, and there are a number of other related frameworks by which people generally study ethics in corporate settings. Academic fields that undergo rapid growth can often become confusing areas. Academic disciplines that are explicitly concerned with improving quality of life and societal concerns in a practical way are often concerned with understanding problems from different perspectives. This means that the solutions and frameworks they provide often overlap, and the problems they stem from evolve at different paces, which means that the prominence of certain approaches and disciplines alters over time. In their outline of the development of evidence-based medicine, for example, Barends *et al* (2012) demonstrate how physicians used to be suspicious of epidemiology (the study of health over large populations) due to its use by non-medical professionals for political purposes. However, with the advent of evidence-based approaches to medicine and medical education, epidemiology's potential to be a key player in clinical diagnoses was realised and it became central to practice.

The field of business ethics has undergone a similar level of development, which has meant that individuals often confuse corporate social responsibility with corporate governance, or sustainability with environmental activities such as recycling or investing in renewable energy sources. In 2008, Mark Schwartz and Archie Carroll helped untangle these many overlapping strands in their article, 'Integrating and unifying competing and complementary frameworks: The search for a common core in the business and society field'. Schwartz & Carroll propose the existence of several frameworks related to the ethics of organisational life that variously compete with and complement each other. Of these frameworks, five have come to the fore:

o Corporate social responsibility;

o Corporate citizenship;

o Stakeholder management;

o Sustainability; and

o Business ethics.

It is possible that you are reading this book because you are currently taking a course that has at least one of these phrases as part of its title. 'Business ethics' is the broader application of ethics to the field of business and is concerned with understanding morality in the context of capitalism and organised/managed labour. It is generally concerned with the application of frameworks and constructs from the fields of moral philosophy and applied ethics to the world of business (such as utilitarianism, deontology, rights, care, justice and virtue).

Most business ethics texts take care to identify the three most influential ethical traditions that have come to dominate contemporary moral philosophy:

o Deontological ethics;

o Consequentialist ethics; and

o Virtue ethics.

Deontological ethics are ethics that are concerned with what *must*, as opposed to *should*, be done. Indeed, the word *deon* is Greek for 'duty', and so deontological ethics is primarily concerned with fulfilling one's duty as the most moral thing to do. The philosopher Immanuel Kant (1724-1804) proposed that the study of duty was the role of ethics. Kant wanted to develop a rational ethics that would be *categorical* (in the sense of being unconditional and would apply to everyone) and *universal* (in that it would apply in all circumstances and without exception). One of Kant's most famous contributions to ethical thought became known as the *categorical imperative*. The two principal aspects of the categorical imperative are:

o Act only on those maxims that you can help make into a universal law;

o Always treat other persons as ends in themselves and never only as means.

Due to its emphasis on rational thinking, deontological ethics has been very influential in academic studies of ethics and is primarily oriented towards the individual, and modernity's interest in the concept of rights.

Consequentialist ethics share the deontological tradition's emphasis on rationalist thinking but, in many ways, it is its opposite. Consequentialism is not as popular in academic discourse, but one of its most obvious products – utilitarianism – is 'probably the most powerful single philosophy in social and economic policy in the modern "Western" world' (Curry, 2011: 44). Utilitarianism advocates attempting to deliver the greatest good (or 'happiness') for the greatest number of people. It advocates deciding what this good or happiness is by calculating whether the result will deliver the most benefits or lowest costs to the largest number of people. As such, it has been used by economists and politicians to determine outcomes for large groups of people.

Utilitarianism and deontological ethics are based on the premise that we can *rationally* assess any situation and make a judgment about how to proceed ethically from that assessment. It is probably not surprising that the impracticality of these approaches became problematic, which led to a return to the oldest system of philosophy in Western thought.

This involved re-evaluating the works of Aristotle (384-322 BC), which had fallen out of fashion as a result of the rise of the deontological and consequentialist schools of thought.

Over the past 200 or so years, *deontological* and *utilitarian* perspectives dominated the field of ethics, but gradually dissatisfaction began to grow with these approaches. In 1958, the British philosopher Elizabeth Anscombe wrote 'Modern moral philosophy', an essay that began a debate about whether it was important to return to roots of moral philosophy following the mistakes of the recent past that had seen some of the supposedly most 'civilised' or 'developed' countries in the world reduced to war and genocide on a scale that had never been seen before. Philosophical rules and utilitarian formulae had not prevented the deaths and displacement of millions during World War II.

The result was a return to the origins of contemporary moral philosophy in ancient Greece where Aristotle (384-322 BC) who, along with making substantial contributions to a variety of fields, had developed some key ethical principles that appeared to have been forgotten in the rush to 'progress' civilisation. In times of crisis, failure or disaster, it is not unusual for theorists to return to Aristotle for grounding; indeed, as the current global financial crisis deepened, some leading figures in European intellectual life urged a re-engagement with Aristotelian principles to help create a new understanding of how management education can create more sustainable business models in the future (Currie *et al*, 2010).

In his *Nicomachean Ethics* (more commonly known amongst philosophers as *Ethics*), Aristotle begins by asserting that everything and everyone has some in-built qualities that make it useful for some ends:

> Every art and every investigation, and similarly every action or pursuit, is considered to aim at some good. Hence the Good has been rightly defined as "that at which all things aim". (1976: 63)

Aristotle saw the aim of the various activities that make up human life as being oriented around one goal: human flourishing or happiness. All things have a purpose (or *telos*). As human beings, we must find two things: our *telos* and the means for achieving our *telos*. To achieve an excellent purpose, you need to employ excellent means. The Greek word that Aristotle used for excellence (*arete*) also translates as virtue. The virtue, then, of any thing is what makes it good at what it is for. An excellent knife is excellent because it is sharp enough for us to cut whatever we want. For humans to have a good life (a life where we can be happy, rather than wealthy at all costs, or solely focused on our personal pleasure), we must be clear about what our virtues are, so we can flourish ourselves and be of service to other people.

Aristotle proposed a *golden mean* to assist us determine our virtues. Too much, or too little, of anything is bad for you and so virtues lie on the mean between extremes of emotion and character. Suppose we are faced with a groupwork situation where we are uncomfortable with the fact that other members of the group are planning to plagiarise the work of students in another module and pass it off as their own. If we decide not to raise our voice in opposition out of fear, then we suffer from a deficiency of virtue, which manifests as the vice of cowardice. We then become more prone to being cowardly in other areas of our life, which ultimately impacts on other people when we become too afraid to stand up for others who are being bullied or oppressed. At the other extreme, we might react angrily and too forcefully, which is a result of an excessive vice. If we allow this to happen too often, we become self-righteous and allow our anger to work its way into parts of our lives where it should have no place. This ultimately results in others suffering as we ourselves become bullies and oppressive in our dealings with other people. The golden mean between these extremes is the virtue of courage, where we calmly and firmly assert our values in a way that assists other people attain this virtue also. The more we practice this virtue, the less we are afraid and less prone to rage. The more a virtue or vice is practiced, the more it becomes settled within our personal disposition and eventually becomes a habit of character. As a habit, virtues help us to moderate our feelings and attitudes in any social context and are then applied to making moral decisions and judgements when the need arises. We attain virtues through consistent practice, and through influencing others to model their behaviour on ours.

It is important to remember that virtues are not just 'nice things to have': they serve a purpose. This return to virtue in contemporary moral philosophy is known as *virtue ethics* and its proponents maintain that human beings are supposed to have lives of well-being, fulfilment and happiness. By practising virtues, we can obtain this life of flourishing for ourselves, and, in turn, help others attain it also. One of the most influential virtue ethicists, Alasdair MacIntyre, states that making an ethical decision about the type of work we do is central to being happy, having a good life and flourishing as individuals (1979).

The Christian element of virtue ethics is found in the theories of St. Thomas Aquinas, who advised people to follow the occupational path that they felt most drawn to, because this was what God wanted them to do: not for their own sake, but because it created social worth for other people. Marx was not anti-vocation, or anti-work, as some commentators have wrongly expressed (indeed, he was a highly prolific and productive writer, scholar and journalist in his own right).

Virtue ethics, then, builds on some of the most influential ethical theories available to us in order to develop new understandings of the relationship that we have with our occupational plans. Whereas rule-based or deontological theories distance us from our ethical dilemmas by providing templates or formulae for resolving moral crises, virtue ethics places ourselves and development of our own character at the centre of understanding our own ethical position. Choosing an occupational path for the wrong reasons (personal gain, money, laziness, self-delusion) is bad because it will impact on our health and human flourishing, producing vices that will ultimately harm us. Choosing and committing to a path based on our real interests and skills that can create value for other people, regardless of the field in which we choose to practice, is key to understanding ourselves and is instrumental to help us start living 'good' lives. Thus, compromising our occupational ambitions might not be as ethically neutral as one might have previously imagined. We will turn to the question of how people can use ethics to think about and find out what type of work they should do in **Chapter 3**.

Business ethicists are specifically interested in morality at:

o **The macro-level:** The influence that social-economic and legal institutions and systems have on the ways that businesses operate;

o **The meso-level:** The activities and behaviours of corporate entities or units or groups within structured companies; and

o **The micro-level:** The values, beliefs and behaviours of individuals within organisations.

It perhaps goes without saying that, during the global financial crisis, attention first focused at the micro-level, with the character and practices of certain managers in particular institutions coming under intense levels of scrutiny as the general public attempted to make sense of how the credit crunch turned into a credit crisis, which then rapidly became a global recession that threatened the fabric of the global financial system. This is not to say that macro-level systemic issues and meso-level corporate issues have not come also under scrutiny, but the initial response to the crisis was certainly one marked by individuals trying to come to terms with *who* rather than *what* 'caused' the crisis and 'how' it was constructed. Studying ethics psychoanalytically involves stepping outside the immediately observable. It means conducting investigations that ask us to consider our selves and our roles in groups, societies and organisations in ways we may never have considered before.

PSYCHOANALYSING THE ETHICS OF ORGANISATIONAL LIFE

Psychoanalysis might appear to be a strange way to study business ethics. Think about what the word 'psychoanalysis' means to you. If it brings to mind a psychiatrist or therapist sitting behind a patient, or a patient lying on a couch, or a group of people sitting in a circle discussing shared problems and challenges, you share the conception that psychoanalysis is mainly used in *therapeutic* settings. This, indeed, is how the discipline and practice of psychoanalysis first emerged in the 19th century, but it was not long before its theories were applied in a range of social sciences and humanities based disciplines.

Psychoanalysis is not one thing. Since Sigmund Freud first used the term in 1896 (Freud, 1974), it has emerged into various schools of thoughts and approaches, but is generally considered to be concerned with understanding the way in which the unconscious works, how it develops and how it impacts on conscious life at the level of the individual, the group and society. Many theorists and therapists remain overtly Freudian in their outlook; many more dissent to various degrees from him and his theories. He is certainly a central figure in the development of psychoanalysis, so any introduction to the topic must discuss his theory as the basis for how it is developed. As the psychiatrist R.D. Laing wrote in his exceptional and compassionate study of schizophrenia, *The Divided Self*:

> Freud was a hero. He descended to the 'Underworld' and met there stark terrors. He carried with him his theory as a Medusa's head which turned these terrors into stone. (1990: 25)

So, what exactly did he do? Freud was a highly controversial character in intellectual circles during his working life, and the impact of his work continues to remain contentious. For example, my bookshelf houses a psychology textbook from the early 1990s that introduces its discussion of Freud's psychoanalytic theory by claiming it to be one of the most un-psychological and unscientific theories ever to exist!

Freud was born into an impoverished Jewish family in the mid-19th century. Academically brilliant in many disciplines, he was fascinated with both the mythical stories of ancient classical religions, and the scientific work of Charles Darwin. Aged 17, he entered the University of Vienna and was soon drawn to the natural sciences. His inquisitive and analytic mindset cannot but have been influenced during this period as a result of his work in laboratories analysing natural specimens. Initially interested in becoming a neurologist, he qualified as a doctor, established a medical practice specialising in nervous diseases and continued to work as a medical researcher. Freud won a fellowship that enabled him to travel to Paris early in his medical career to study with Jean-Martin Charcot, who had achieved fame as a pioneer in the field of hypnosis. Charcot's lectures on hypnosis (which he was using to treat what was known as 'hysteria') often involved demonstrations of the effects of hypnosis on patients.

Observing Charcot applying hypnotism allowed Freud to realise that a considerable part of human consciousness was actually unconscious. How else could a hypnotist 'suggest' to a patient that they do something at a level that they were not already conscious of. And this is perhaps the greatest single contribution of Freud to the development of the social sciences: just as we develop consciously through our lives, we also develop at an unconscious level. Unlike our conscious thoughts however, our unconscious is chaotic, disorganised and inconsistent. The unconscious is full of drives, neurosis, fears, desires and urges over which we have no control. Freud proposed that the unconscious is not immediately accessible to us. This is because our psyche protects us from acting on the destructive whims of the unconscious by repressing them. Hypnotism was one way to access the unconscious, but Freud sought other ways 'in'. He applied a 'talking-cure' that had been pioneered by a colleague, which allowed patients to 'free-associate' responses to questions from analysts. These provided important clues to the contents of fears and anxieties that were repressed in the unconscious. The contents of dreams, long ignored by rational science as psychic waste, was seen as highly valuable material where the unconscious could be observed in its true uncoordinated and contradictory state. Dreams, according to Freud, were attempts by the psyche to fulfil our unconscious wishes and desires. Because of their non-linear and fluid nature, dreams (and the wishes they contain) need to be *interpreted* according to the individual's experiences. Dreams, when analysed properly, have the potential to tell us what our real motivations and desires are, particularly, according to Freud, when we find these interpretations distasteful: in fact, our attempts to distance ourselves from uncomfortable analyses of our dreams mirrors the way that the *ego* and *superego* try to suppress our instinctual desires. A slightly more conscious way of determining how the *id* influences the objects and achievements that individuals are motivated by is to examine the content of *daydreams,* which usually consist of *fantasies* that the individual harbours.

Towards the end of his career, Freud proposed that the psyche is a dynamic collection of desires, drives and impulses that actively influence how we, as individuals, think and behave. The psyche (or mind), according to Freud, is structured in the following way:

o The *id* is made up of uncoordinated instinctual trends that operate in uncontrolled ways on our thinking and behaviour. Present from the moment of birth, the *id* demands that our most primal instincts and impulses be satisfied. Think of the *id* as your inner 'baby'. If a baby is hungry, it *demands* to be fed immediately and ignores the needs of others around it;

o The *ego* is the organised 'realistic' part of the mind that recognises reality and works on the *id* to control its behaviour. The *ego* is the *id* grown up. Children no longer make unrealistic demands of their caregivers when they recognise that the resources are unavailable to satisfy impulses (such as hunger);

o The *superego* is the critical and moralising part of the mind. Its psychic function is to help us develop as good people in relation to the communities that we are part of. The *superego* is the part of our mind that works with the culture in which we find ourselves in order to ensure that we do not end up acting on the whims of the *id*, which would result in chaos:

> Thus, civilization has to be defended against the individual, and its regulations, institutions and commands are directed to that task ... It seems rather that every civilization must be built up on coercion and renunciation of instinct. (Freud, 2001: 7)

This is not to say that, over the course of our development, the *id* gets quieter and is gradually replaced by the *ego*, which in turn is subsumed by the *superego*. In fact, Freud proposed that the opposite actually happens: the *id* tries to monopolise all our mental energy in order to satisfy our instincts, and the *ego* and *superego* have to work hard to control this energy.

Freud creates a picture of the mind as something conflicted between various forces that seek gratification in particular ways. Freud saw the drive for sexual gratification as fundamental to how he configured his contribution to psychology as a field of study, and to psychoanalysis as a therapeutic practice, but this belief has been challenged by a number of psychoanalysts. Freud writes about motivation from a psychoanalytical perspective that is not generally discussed in the mainstream of organisational behaviour, which tends to be concerned with creating structures or circumstances that can motivate people to work in different ways. Psychoanalysis tells us that our unconscious *works* on our conscious thoughts in an active way.

However, Freud raises some interesting questions about motivation in highlighting that individuals are driven to satisfy needs that they may not be consciously aware of, or have tried to suppress. Mistakes (which Freud calls *parapraxes*), such as 'slips of the tongue', 'slips of the pen' or forgetting, are messages from parts of the mind that we are not conscious of, that we are doing something that does not match what the *id* needs at a particular point in time. Mistakes, according to Freud, fulfil wishes that we are not consciously aware of (Freud, 1974). In 1901, he published a highly influential book, *The Psychopathology of Everyday Life*, which demonstrated that everybody's unconscious plays a much greater role in our daily lives than anyone had predicted beforehand. This could be interpreted as psychoanalysis's first trip outside the analyst's consulting room into the real world of everyday work and family life. Psychoanalysis stops being just for doctors and patients, but for everyone interested in people and how they live and work together.

Freud was a prolific and lucid writer, so it is possible to trace the evolution of his thought throughout his long career. He had much to say about clinical problems in relation to neurosis, aggression, anxiety, sexuality, ethics and morality and some of these theoretical contributions will be referred to alongside those of his followers who developed them, throughout this text. It is important to note that, although Freud was concerned with the inner world of the individual of which they themselves may not have been fully conscious, Freud was very interested in how the unconscious formed, and was formed by the social and the institutional. His idea of a 'psychodynamic' mind referred to the way that forces in one part of the mind might influence and impact on another, but it also demonstrates how external forces can shape the unconscious and *vice versa*. Throughout his career, he became increasingly interested in groups, organisations, institutions and society. The First World War and the rise of the Nazis (who eventually drove him and his family from his beloved Vienna) provided a whole new set of symptoms and social concerns requiring psychoanalysis. Although much of Freud's later writing attempted to engage with those directly traumatised by these large-scale horrors, a significant proportion of it was concerned with how large groups of people came to participate in organised movements that led to unprecedented levels of human suffering.

Many theorists have rejected Freud's work on the basis that there is not enough evidence to back-up his concepts, and that they are inherently sexist and male-oriented, or that they are universalistic and play down the important role of culture. Nevertheless, it is important when attempting to understand his work, particularly in relation to our occupational and organisational ambitions, to realise that motivation is not something necessarily driven by external factors, but is often deeply embedded within an individual's personal experience. Because parts of our psyche work to censor our instinctual drives and desires, at a personal level the driving forces behind our motivations are obscured from our own view. Even when we are at rest, there is much work underway deep within our unconscious minds.

Osnos (2011) writes that public fascination with psychoanalysis as a therapeutic practice peaked during the 1950s and by the 1970s had gone into decline as result of new therapeutic or pharmaceutical innovations. One of the most famous of these has been the growth of a therapeutic approach known as Cognitive Behavioural Therapy (or CBT). Whereas psychoanalysis is often expensive, interpretive and can take a long time, CBT is fast and efficient in helping patients to address patterns of thought that result in negative emotions. In many health systems, CBT has become the therapeutic method of choice for health policy-makers and economists because it is cheaper than psychoanalysis. Burkeman (2016) demonstrates that one of the central differences between CBT and psychoanalysis is that the former tries to alleviate one symptom with a view to eliminating it, whereas psychoanalysis uses these symptoms to try to develop a more comprehensive picture of the individual's unconscious life.

Another reason for the supposed decline of psychoanalysis has been the rapid rise of awareness of the field of neuroscience, which is a collection of scientific fields that variously study the human brain. Freud began his career as a neurologist, seeking to scientifically discover the inner-depths of the human mind. Many have claimed that recent scientific discoveries about the human brain will fundamentally change our understanding of our species, while others believe these claims to be hugely overstated. In a brilliant book, *Neuro,* which explored the huge growth of awareness of the field of neuroscience (a growth that Tallis [2012] has referred to as 'neuromania'), Nikolas Rose and Joelle Abi-Rached (2013) demonstrate the economic, technological and social forces that have led to a general familiarity with neuroscience that has grown rapidly since the 1960s to a point where many advocate it as being a core field for understanding who we are, how we should behave and how we should be governed. It is worth remembering that similar expectations were placed on psychoanalysis during its ascendency. Rose and Abi-Rached (2013) demonstrate that the way '*psy-*' was attached to a diverse range of unrelated fields up to around 50 years ago is now occurring with the prefix '*neuro-*'. This has resulted in whole new set of fields, including neuro-law; neuro-finance; neuro-economics; neuro-marketing; neuro-anthropology, neuro-ergonomics; neuro-theology; neuro-ethics; neuro-education; neuro-entrepreneurship, etc. By the time you've finished reading this paragraph, a new '*neuro-*' may have emerged! It is interesting to note that surprisingly little research has been published on the ethics of business and work from a neuroscientific perspective, and much that has tends to query whether its application in fields such as leadership or marketing is ethical (Duta *et al,* 2011; Farah, 2012; Zimmerman & Racine, 2012; Flores *et al,* 2014).

If the vast majority of neuroscientists are reluctant to make claims other than what they can empirically prove, why has it become a field that manifests so strongly in public consciousness? One of the key reasons is that one of the central drivers of its growth has been the emergence of neuroimaging technologies that made the living brain visible for the first time in the 1970s and 1980s. As the publicity departments of research centres, hospitals and universities released new findings to the press, it was possible to accompany these with vivid graphs and photographs, which enhanced the 'sell-ability' of the new discoveries for general consumption. Just as economics has the potential to feed new data and theories to the business sections of newspapers on a regular basis (Cullen, 2008), neuroscience has the same ability to provide fresh insights about human behaviour to the general and lifestyle sections. Watch out for the next news item you encounter beginning with the words, 'neuroscientists have discovered ...'. Psychoanalysis, with its more interpretive and processual method is a far less 'media-friendly' discipline.

The ascendency of neuroscience, however, should not be taken to mean that it is in any way in competition with psychoanalysis. Neuroscience studies the brain; psychoanalysis studies the psyche. Indeed, Burkeman (2016) writes that some neuroscientists have found that the brain can process information at a much faster pace than we can be aware, and we still don't know what much of it is doing! There is much more going outside the conscious parts of our psyches than we can hope to know.

Others have raised concerned about the lack of evidence of whether psychoanalysis works as a therapy, but this in itself ignores a crucial fact. Psychoanalysts, unlike social or experimental psychologists, are bound by an oath of secrecy towards their patients and so cannot share the results of their findings in the same way that researchers can. Indeed, Freud went to considerable lengths to disguise the cases he discussed in his theories with pseudonyms. Many people who enter psychoanalysis as a therapeutic measure in contemporary times do so on the understanding that they will guaranteed absolute anonymity. Such an arrangement is clearly an impediment to sharing evidence about the successes of psychoanalysis as a therapy. Because therapies such as CBT measure whether a particular symptom has been eliminated, it is easier to construct empirical evidence of whether they have worked. Only recently has evidence been collected in a more systematic way on the outcomes of psychoanalysis, and Shedler (2010) has shown that there is a large evidence-base for psychoanalytic approaches being more effective in providing longer-term solutions to mental health problems than other forms of therapies.

One of the main reasons why psychoanalysis doesn't get discussed or reported on as much as neuroscience, CBT or economics is because of its success in entering the general repertoire of how we understand the word today. Mention the words 'therapy' or 'psychoanalysis' to anyone and they will probably immediately conjure up images of bearded, cigar-smoking analysts or the consulting couch associated with Freud. The language of psychoanalysis has permeated contemporary discourse; words such as 'obsessive', 'neurotic', 'complex', 'narcissist' or 'projection' are used and understood by people in all sections of society. In other words, we don't notice psychoanalytic terminology or concepts anymore because they are everywhere! In the director's commentary to *A Dangerous Method* (2012), David Cronenberg describes a scene where Sigmund Freud and Carl Jung discuss psychoanalysis as involving the creation of the 20th century and modern relationships where people have been freed to discuss their inner lives to an extent that would have been reprehensible before. This movement has led to the development of more intimate conversations right throughout professional and social relationships all throughout the world. In a sense, psychoanalysis fundamentally changed the nature of friendship and intimacy, as well as our relationship with our unconscious lives.

Although psychoanalysis may have become of less interest to healthcare policy-makers, it has a longstanding influence on the humanities and cultural studies. For example, many prominent public intellectuals, such as Slavoj Zizek, practice a form of cultural and political analysis that is primarily psychoanalytic. More recently, however, psychoanalysis has increasingly been used by people who research and theorise about businesses, the corporate sector and organisations.

In a *Financial Times* interview (Wallace, 2009), a psychoanalyst, who solved a number of workplace problems by applying a variant of psychoanalysis (known as socioanalysis) to real management and workplace problems, highlighted that practitioners of psychoanalysis often focus on solving problems faced in their personal, rather than working, lives. This appears to be changing: the Showtime television show, *Billions*, for example, has a central character who is a trained psychiatrist who analyses, counsels and coaches hedge fund employees. She is clearly a central figure in the hedge fund and reflects the real existence of practitioners of psychoanalysis in companies where employee underperformance can result in the loss of huge sums of money for clients. It is also made clear that she is more than a motivational coach; she uses psychoanalysis to understand the unique unconscious desires and fears of her clients to help them overcome their neuroses and enable them to succeed.

One of the foremost contemporary figures in the application of psychoanalytic theory to developing new understandings of the practical world of work and organisations is Professor Yiannis Gabriel. In a recent book chapter, he recounts the history of how psychoanalysis has impacted our understanding of workplaces in two main ways. The first is the direct application of psychoanalytic theory to the problems faced by managers, employees and consultants working in, and with, business organisations (Gabriel & Carr, 2002). The second way in which psychoanalysis has changed our understanding of workplaces has been through its application to the artefacts, events and practices in organisations to generate new forms of theories of how we work together. As such, psychoanalysis has much to tell us about real organisational issues at managerial, strategic, group and operational levels, such as failures, power, bullying, discrimination, culture, whistleblowing, leadership, etc. It can be used interpretively or critically to understand the problems or issues that impact individuals and groups, which they themselves may not understand. When one considers how workplaces attempt to manage and control the behaviours of individuals with diverse goals, it is perhaps not surprising how other results usually manifest. Many of the moral or normalising forces that are present in the workplace are visible only at a surface level. Psychoanalytic studies of business ethics attempt to understand what happens underneath what an organisation says it wants at an unconscious level.

STUDYING ETHICS, WORK & ORGANISATIONAL LIFE

You will notice from the above that a number of different academic approaches and schools of thought are used to study ethics. This book is structured to take these into account along the various stages of a 'typical' working life, from the time one chooses the type of work that we do, to entering an organisation or starting a business, to moving into management. To do this, however, we must first look at the context in which business is currently undertaken.

This means that the next chapter in this book will examine contemporary theories and critiques of capitalism, and how current iterations of it impact on people's working lives.

Having outlined some of the main classic and contemporary theories in this field, we will then turn to examining ethics from the perspective of new employees (**Chapter 3**), established employees and members of organisational cultures (**Chapter 4**), and managers (**Chapter 5**).

Having discussed these perspectives, we then move on to look at how organisations variously 'do' ethics. The first of these chapters (**Chapter 6**) will examine strategic approaches to ethics, particularly the influence of stakeholder theory. **Chapter 7** will then outline developments in relation to corporate practices such as corporate social responsibility, corporate citizenship and corporate governance. **Chapter 8** will examine the critical relationship of ecological ethics with organisations, while **Chapter 9** will focus on international business theory and the responsibilities of organisations working in a globalised market. The final chapter in the book will examine leadership as an ethical construct. Most of the established theory in areas such as corporate social responsibility, corporate citizenship and corporate governance tends to focus on how initiatives are done *to* employees, markets and customers from the top down. Psychoanalysis can help us understand what individuals and groups do *to* these concepts.

This book takes ethics and organisational life as 'lived' concepts, which means that we should not only focus on what businesses, organisations and managers 'should do'; we also need to understand why they sometimes act in unethical or self-destructive ways to ensure that we, as employees or managers, do not make the same mistakes that others have made in the past. Doing this means that we must reach beyond a single disciplinary framework. As such, this approach is primarily psychoanalytical in its approach, but psychoanalysis in turn frequently informs and engages with theories that have been developed in the field of cultural psychology, management theory, moral philosophy, political theory, psychoanalysis, social psychology and sociology. The field of business ethics is in no way 'fixed' and all of these approaches are used in the peer-reviewed research literature on a variety of these topics.

Ethical theory on work, organisations and business constantly changes, and this book aims to act as an introduction to the field of study. Many theories from a variety of disciplinary areas are mentioned throughout the text, but these *mentions* cannot explain their full depth. With this in mind, towards the end of the text, a short chapter of *Further Reading* is provided to assist readers to explore these ideas in more detail.

2: CAPITALISM: CHAMPIONS & CRITICS

At the nexus of business, ethics and society lies one of the most enduring concepts that has shaped life in the modern era: capital. Capital is not just about finance, investing or accounting. Capitalism is more than solely economically-based. We might define it as assets and resources possessed by a person, group or organisation that can be deployed to gain additional resources or other advantages. The French sociologist Pierre Bourdieu proposed (1990) that capital also operated at a social level, which could lead to varied types of success, depending on the forms of capital that were available to individuals in particular settings.

To understand how this happens, it is important to explain two discrete concepts. The first of these is 'habitus', which is the way in which we as individuals deal with the world. Our 'mental maps' and programmed behaviour are so much an element of our day-to-day lives that we often fail to appreciate that other people share them. We (along with our habitus) enter into various social fields constantly and attempt to use the capital available to us to change the field or to gain an advantage within it (Ritzer, 1996). The second concept is that of 'the field'. Fields are discrete networks of relationships that exist apart from us as individuals (such as membership of elite groups, jobs with impressive companies, places on prestigious teams, etc.).

Bourdieu identified four main forms of capital that individuals could use to gain an advantage in a particular field. **Economic capital** is the way in which most people use the term 'capital': in its most basic form, this means money. We derive **social capital** from membership or access to elite groups, while **cultural capital** is the name Bourdieu gives to the knowledge, skills and credentials that enable us to move to our advantage within specific fields. Cultural capital can be obtained from our friends or family, but is best accessed through education. As such, it allows us to think, move, dress, speak and act in a way that will gain us access to specific fields in which we want to operate and succeed.

Bourdieu identified three sub-forms of cultural capital that we could 'grow' through our engagement in the education system and then use for our advantage in selected fields: *embodied* cultural capital (capital that we carry around with us in our ways of thinking, speaking, even moving); *objectified* cultural capital (which we gain through the material possession of important symbolic items); and *institutionalised* cultural capital (such as educational qualifications that can be easily translated into economic capital in the labour market).

When all these forms of capital are combined, they amount to **symbolic capital** (prestige, honour or status) that allows the holder to dominate people who do not possess the same amount of symbolic capital. This domination usually happens in ways in which the subordinate party is complicit (or even expects) through acts of 'symbolic violence'. Symbolic, cultural and social capital can all be traded in the same manner as economic capital. For example, individuals might 'trade' their cultural capital for economic capital in a job interview or contract.

The usefulness of the concept of capital has led to it being used in a variety of organisational contexts. Human capital, for example, has been used in organisational studies to represent the combined stock of knowledge, practices and habits, culture and capacity for innovation and change that gives an organisation advantages over competitors. Related to human capital is the concept of intellectual capital, which is a combination of the intellectual property held by a business and the number of people in the company who can increase this capital. Such resources are not necessarily economically 'calculable' but are nevertheless of enormous value to organisations, particularly those operating in more knowledge-intensive environments. Because these forms of capital are intangible and can never truly be owned by the organisation due to being *part* of the individuals working for the organisation, businesses often work to retain key individuals by offering them rewards that assist those individuals in turn to increase their economic, social, cultural and symbolic capital.

Recently, scholars studying gender in the workplace have demonstrated how gender is a form of capital that can be variously used in work contexts (Huppatz, 2010, 2012; Huppatz & Goodwin, 2013). Popular management bookshelves often stock books that claim to have discovered new forms of capital such as 'spiritual capital' (Zohar & Marshall, 2005) or more controversially, 'erotic capital' (Hakim, 2011).

VARIETIES OF CAPITALISM

Since the Industrial Revolution in the 19th century, capitalism has become the most widespread and dynamic system of economic organisation in history. Ingham (2008) identified the three core elements required for capitalism as:

o A monetary system that can finance enterprise through debt and/or speculation;

o The existence of markets for exchanging different forms of capital or commodities; and

o The production of commodities by private enterprise.

The technological innovations brought about during the Industrial Revolution radically changed the way that production and consumption 'happened'. Huge population increases in urban centres were accompanied by large-scale rural depopulation, which radically and permanently changed the social and physical landscape of countries impacted by it. Concerned with the negative impact of the new factory system on the poor, Marx published *Capital* in 1860. Marx's detailed and complex analysis (1995) posited the existence of an eternal struggle between labour (the workers) and capital (the owners of the means of production). Free trade and globalisation accelerated over the course of the 19th and 20th centuries, leading eventually to the first major global depression in the early 20th century. The 'New Deal' proposed by US President Roosevelt was the first large-scale attempt to tame what Adam Smith (1970) had referred to as the 'invisible hand' of the market through government intervention. This intervention was gradually challenged over the years until the early 1970s, when many governments (such as in the UK, the US, China and Chile) advocated overturning the social element of economic policy to restore market-oriented economic systems. Hall & Soskice (2001) propose that there are varieties of capitalism, such as *liberal market economies*, where firms co-ordinate their activities in competitive market settings, and *co-ordinated market economies*, where firms co-ordinate their activities in relation to other firms and non-market actors. A relatively new form of capitalism has been named 'state capitalism' (Williams, 1988; Ingham, 2008), which describes commercial ventures and investing activities undertaken by governments that are publicly owned or controlled by their workers.

When governments embrace such pro-capital policies, they are embracing an ideology known as *neo-liberalism*. Neo-liberalism has been described in a variety of different ways, but one of the best-known theorists, geographer David Harvey (2005), proposed that it consists of a group of economic and political policies and practices based on the belief that human well-being is best achieved in an environment where freedom to trade, participate in markets, set up businesses (or sell skills to businesses) is guaranteed by governments that offer strong protections to the rights of groups and individuals to own private property.

Many governments gradually adopted neo-liberal policies from the early 1970s right up until the emergence of the current crisis (Fukuyama, 1992). Because people are understandably averse to sacrificing their quality of life to serve other people's desire for capitalistic accumulation, governments that wish to follow this path, it has been claimed, deploy 'shock tactics' to reinforce neo-liberal policies that prioritise the rights of private citizens and businesses over the collective good (Klein, 2008). However, it may be inaccurate to declare that neo-liberalism has replaced traditional capitalism, as many governments often try to capture the benefits of capitalism without sacrificing social responsibilities.

CHAMPIONS & CRITICS OF CAPITALISM

Many influential theorists and economists have argued for various forms of capitalism over others. Liberal and neo-liberal economic activists, such as Milton Friedman, supported Adam Smith's claim that, as individuals, we are primarily motivated by self-interest and greed above all other emotions.

In *The Wealth of Nations*, Smith (1970) states a moral rationale for capitalism: when individuals satisfy their private needs through participating in markets, public welfare increases. In other words, the richer people get through capitalistic behaviour, the more wealth they create for others, and through contributing to systems of taxation, in turn generate more resources to address the welfare needs of disadvantaged sectors of society. Most importantly, Smith articulated a belief, which has become widely held, that individuals are primarily self-interested utility-maximisers. In other words, we are motivated to work solely in order to accumulate more goods for ourselves. Because of this, we feel the force of the market in all our dealings with other people, a phenomenon that Smith named 'the invisible hand of market competition'. More recently, this process of economisation, where individuals are encouraged to see every aspect of their life solely in financial or economic terms, has been the subject of extensive critique (Martin, 2002; Hochschild, 1983, 2003; Cullen, 2008a, 2015; Monbiot, 2016).

Smith's ideas have been at loggerheads with Marx's critique of capitalism for centuries: Smith believed that markets were systems that could best benefit individuals as they moved towards a state of perfect competition; Marx believed that markets were inherently immoral, as they represented a distorted view of morality and human behaviour that was alien to the human's 'authentic' nature. Both ideas have been highly influential in debates about the best way to structure and govern the societies in which we live.

In *The Road to Serfdom*, Friedrich Hayek (1976) wrote that any attempt to regulate markets through centralised planning by governments would ultimately result in losses of freedom and welfare across all sections of society, including the disadvantaged. Hayek believed that governments had a responsibility to promote the freest form of markets possible, as this was the most efficient way to govern the economy of any country. Karl Polanyi (1957) later demonstrated how the rise of the modern nation-state became intertwined with the emergence of market economies. Polanyi posited that the modern state was needed to push changes in social structure that allowed for a competitive capitalist economy, and simultaneously that capitalism required a strong legal state that would mitigate the harsher effects of this transformation. In short, our idea of what it means to be an effective citizen in a modern liberal democracy is intertwined with capitalism. Polanyi proposed his famous 'double movement' idea, which claimed that, once free markets attempt to separate from society, social protectionism would come into play.

Recent critiques of capitalism have focused on the way it has been enforced in an increasingly global way. Klein (2008) demonstrated how economic downturns and natural disasters were increasingly used to exploit the people who had been injured by them, in a process known as *disaster capitalism*. When people are shocked or disoriented as a result of a crisis, some business people use the opportunity to buy up previously costly resources at highly discounted rates. At a structural level, disaster capitalism allows governments to introduce economic shock therapy: when people are at their weakest, changes to governance structures, employment rights legislation and contractual agreements can be introduced in a way that would have not be accepted prior to a 'shock'. David Harvey (2005) has accounted for the way in which legislation designed to protect these rights, which was introduced in the aftermath of the Great Depression, had been seen by many capitalists as an impediment to growth. Since the mid-1970s, many governments have worked against these principles in order to gradually reduce the role of the state in contemporary life so that the laws of the market can increasingly take precedence.

To summarise, champions of capitalism claim its benefits to be that it:

o Incentivises freedom;

o Adapts to changing social circumstances;

o Generates wealth and employment for many;

o Appeals to the belief that human beings are primarily motivated by self-interest.

The downsides of capitalism, according to its critics, are that it:

o Creates too much choice and freedom, which distracts people from values;

o Generates constant social crises;

o Provides wealth for the wealthy at the expense of the poor;

o Punishes those who work to help others.

When these two general sets of perspectives on capitalism are taken into account, it might be stated that capitalism has been favoured in developed economies (and increasingly, in economies that want to develop) because it has proven to be one of the most efficient ways in which to organise a society. The key difficulty with this statement is that certain groups benefit from these efficiencies at the expense of others.

Why, then, do people participate in a system that does not always benefit them? Why do we sustain a system that we often find to be ethically dubious? There are a number of theories that discuss how capitalism has become part of our unconscious lives, and two of these are explored in the following sections of this chapter. The first of these, 'The Civilizing of Capital', looks at how social and political changes gradually fostered the development of a way of being (or habitus) or living our lives in the world that favours capitalism. The final section, 'Spirits of Capitalism', discusses the religious roots of capitalism and the spiritual reasons for both its initial spread and its ongoing persistence.

THE CIVILIZING OF CAPITAL

Throughout this this text, we will examine the work of thinkers who have attempted to demonstrate how large-scale social or political changes have impacted on our unconscious lives. One of the key figures in helping us understand these processes is the sociologist Norbert Elias, particularly his two-volume study, *The Civilizing Process*, which was published as two separate works in German in 1939, *The History of Manners* (1978) and *State Formation & Civilisation* (1982). If one's superego keeps our behaviour in check by preventing us from behaving in certain ways (either by making us anxious about being perceived a certain way, or by being tortured by our guilt if we have violated a standard set by ourselves or others), Elias demonstrated how it could be influenced by external social processes.

Elias studied how social stabilisation was achieved when power, wealth and the laws centralised around one institution. The emergence of absolute monarchies was vital to this process, as it meant that competing interests in society were governed by a monarch's court. The nobles who were part of this court became important in helping the civilising process throughout society because of their special status and proximity to the absolute power of the monarch. As this continued throughout the Middle Ages, more stable societies resulted in population growth and a desire to live closer to the centres of power and commerce. Because people lived more closely together in a more interdependent fashion, a need emerged for greater physical restraint. If individuals living closely together acted on their physical and psychological impulses in an unrestrained way, chaos would ensue.

Elias studied how these changes were brought into effect by studying the sources that attempt to socialise rules for behaviour when interacting with each other. The study of these 'manuals' and other writings give a very clear picture of the behaviours that were once considered normal and natural, but could no longer be tolerated in a society where people were under increasing pressure to self-regulate their behaviour. These included rules about table manners, spitting, aggression, nose-blowing, aggression, bedroom and sleeping etiquette, bodily functions, and family and marital relationships. Elias refers to these activities moving 'behind the scenes' of social life with the result that the threshold of shame and embarrassment rises, and people become more observant of the behaviour of other people. In other words, what was previously seen as natural, non-remarkable or pleasurable has been forced into one's private life. If we seek a contemporary example of the civilising process, we might look to research exploring the extent to which children and teenagers engage in activities that shame their peers when they fail to wear brands that have been deemed as socially desirable by their peers. Elias gave much time to discussing the importance of teaching rules about 'manners' to children, which in turn influenced the development of the superego. Elias is very clear that civilising is an ongoing practice that influences the individual psyche, alongside significant social change that requires people to live their lives and think of their behaviour in different ways. Elias' civilising process had a huge influence on the development of sociological concepts such as 'disposition' and 'habitus', particularly as discussed by Pierre Bourdieu.

Bourdieu uses the idea of a *disposition* to describe how we learn to 'be' in a given field. A disposition refers to our inclination to think of life, relationships and other groups of people (even the way we express our personality or how we dress, adorn and hold our physical selves) that influence our behaviour. Dispositions are the internal scripts that we have learned from others around us. Because of this, they replicate the social structures of our immediate environment. The *habitus* is a system of these dispositions that exists in a particular field, which not only produces particular forms of action but also sustains cultural practices. Karen Ho's 2009 ethnography of Wall Street, *Liquidated* (which will be discussed in **Chapter 4**), theorises how the habitus of Wall Street investment bankers was constructed through daily practices that include the universities they are recruited from, the hours they work and even the way that they consume their lunch! All of these contribute, according to Ho, to a system that supports the generation of constant financial crises.

SPIRITS OF CAPITALISM

Karl Marx's analysis of how capitalism worked as a system highlighted how industrialisation produced a mode of existence for many workers that was based on pure misery. Towards the end of Chapter 7 of *Capital*, Marx (1995) delivered a famous diatribe against the injustices that capitalist modes of production bring to lives of ordinary employees. He painted a vivid picture of what life had become for many people working in factories in the 19th century, full of evocative words such as 'domination', 'exploitation' and 'mutilation'. By the late 19th and early 20th century, the German sociologist Max Weber had turned his attention to the reasons why people continued to dedicate their lives to working in the capitalist system, especially when it offered them no specific pleasure or enjoyment. Marx had opened the *Communist Manifesto* with the words: 'A spectre is haunting Europe – the spectre of communism' (Marx & Engels, 2004). Against this 'spectre', Weber proposed that that capitalism was successful because it provided people with a 'spirit' that shaped a way for people to find eternal salvation though capitalist work.

Religion has played an enormous role in the development of the contemporary capitalistic world, and the first major study to outline why this is the case was provided by the German sociologist Max Weber in the early 20th century. Rather than assuming work and business activity to be a field of social practice that was dissociated from (or even polar to) the world of transcendent spirituality, Weber saw a direct correlation between the Protestant values and behaviours that drove the development of capitalism. Weber's *The Protestant Ethic and The Spirit of Capitalism* (1992) provides a lucid account of how this impacted on the ways in which people think and conceive of their work in contemporary capitalistic society. Weber sees modern capitalism as oriented around the continuous acquisition of economic wealth for its own sake, rather than for the benefits that this wealth can bring. Weber was interested in why certain regions of Europe had grown more prosperous than others since the Industrial Revolution, and particularly why these regions tended to be 'more Protestant', and why impoverished countries were 'more Catholic'.

Catholicism's primary focus on attaining salvation in the afterlife depended on activities such as acquiring indulgences, confessing sin, and participating in organised sacramental activities that involved removing oneself from the mundane world through forms of prayer, which was celebrated in the monastic ideal.

Protestantism's challenge to Catholicism involved placing a stronger sense of personal responsibility on the individual for ensuring that they were productive individuals. Calvin's version of Protestantism, and its doctrine of predetermination, attempted to undo the technique of repentance and forgiveness that was found in the Catholic sacramental practice of confession. Instead, the believer's access to Heaven was not something they could 'fix' with the assistance of a priest; instead, their salvation was predetermined before birth. Where the Catholic faith system expected and facilitated moral imperfection, Calvinism expected perfection in the lived behaviour of the 'saved'.

If a person is predetermined to go to Heaven or Hell after death, regardless of their behaviour, we might imagine that this would grant individuals a certain amount of freedom in how they chose to conduct themselves in the world. But, according to Weber, this was not the case. Weber states that a key way for believers to get this assurance was to engage in productive worldly activity because the world exists for the glory of God. In Catholicism, one could gain 'points' through indulgences, good works, and repentance; in Protestantism, where one must constantly monitor oneself in order to remain convinced of one's membership of the 'saved', the believer could only *lose* points for less than saintly behaviour. The believer, then, must live a highly productive life in *this* world, accumulating wealth only as an indication that they are among those whom God has elected to save, and unemotionally re-investing it in a way that increases self-assurance of their predetermined path to Heaven.

The Protestant work ethic provided a form of selfhood that aligned with the requirements of modern capitalism: a will to re-invest rather than spend or squander, and a cool, financialised rationality. This selfhood had its foundation in a faith system that led to areas populated by devout Protestants quickly rising within the economic ascendancy, and this 'spirit' continued to prosper for the next 100 years after Weber first proposed it, even when the belief system that underpinned it went into gradual abeyance.

Business and capitalism underwent significant change over the 20th century, so what has happened to the spirit of capitalism since Weber first conceptualised it over a century ago? In 1999, Luc Boltanski & Eve Chiapello published a highly influential work, *The New Spirit of*

Capitalism (translated into English in 2005). In it, Boltanski & Chiapello attempted to map out how the 'spirit of capitalism', which Weber saw as the key spiritual element that drove industrial endeavour amongst certain Protestant congregations, had changed over the course of the 20th century. Boltanski & Chiapello found that this spirit of capitalism changed as a result of social, economic or political crises that caused individuals to rapidly reappraise their theories.

Following such shocks, the spirit of capitalism changed by addressing the problems inherent in capitalism that had caused a particular shock and absorbing these critiques in a new spirit. For example, the shock of the Great Depression in the 1930s signalled the end of many small family-owned firms and was replaced by a *second* spirit that favoured the community ethos that was fostered in large, bureaucratic firms. The second spirit of capitalism was described as a 'social ethic', expertly described in Whyte's *The Organization Man* (1961). As with all spirits of capitalism, the changes that workers and managers engaged with ultimately resulted in a new set of problems that provided the rationale for the emergence of another shock. The organisational community spirit demanded firm allegiance and a sense of conservatism that many ultimately found stifling. The counter-culture of the 1960s led to many of the legal and political customs of post-World War II society in Europe and the US being challenged from within. With the moral basis of Western 'values' being increasingly questioned, governments became concerned about the future of the institutions that underpinned life in the global powerhouses of capitalism.

The problems that led to the emergence of this shock were resolved by the emergence of a *third* spirit of capitalism that led to a spiritualised form of 'soft capitalism' (Heelas & Woodhead, 2005; Cullen, 2009) that was nourished by New Age, person-focused forms of work and organisation (Heelas, 1996; Bell & Taylor, 2004; Cullen, 2008a). This spirit of capitalism saw work as a means of creative self-expression and part of the individual's quest to find their 'authentic self'.

What impact has the recent global financial crisis had on this new spirit of capitalism? How has capitalism absorbed the critiques of it as a system that emerged during one of the most significant challenges that it has undergone? The 'Occupy' movement that sprung up in major cities around the world provided a focal point for many critics of capitalism to converge and declare its imminent demise. Texts continue to appear regularly predicting a doomsday scenario for capitalism (Zizek, 2011; Mason, 2015) but Boltanski & Chiapello's analysis demonstrated that capitalism's mutable nature makes such predictions (despite the high quality of the analyses) questionable.

Eve Chiapello (2013) has written that criticisms of capitalism have always had the power to change it. When criticisms grow, they have the potential to produce situations where ungovernability manifests. Criticism thus can produce ideas for how things might be done differently. The reason for this, as Chiapello lucidly explains, is that successful criticisms of capitalism are usually taken on board and adopted *by capitalism*. Capitalism thus is excellent at absorbing and incorporating the value systems of its own enemies. Unrelated to these points about the highly adaptive nature of the spirit of capitalism, Chiapello also points out that capitalism is able to mobilise itself to areas where the criticism does not exist, is not considered valid, or is not allowed to be vocalised.

The ethical implications of this final point will be discussed in **Chapter 9**. Chiapello (2013), interestingly, analyses the grounds on which criticisms of capitalism are usually made. These usually address the phenomena these 'criticisms actually denounce, and the value system that underpins the critical position from which the critique is being made'.

When taken together, four main critiques of capitalism are identifiable. The first of these is a *social* criticism, familiar to most people, in which capitalism is condemned as being a source of poverty and alienation, where workers are exploited by capitalists. Class differences are reinforced and inequality flourishes as a result of the spread of capitalist values. The second critique is a *conservative* criticism, which is less concerned with what capitalism imposes on workers, but rather with what it does for the established moral order of a society. By creating classes of newly-rich entrepreneurs, capitalism has the potential to disturb the basis by which established elites (classes, owners, churches, political parties, etc.) justify their hold on power. The third criticism is an *artistic* criticism of capitalism, which sees capitalism as productive of a form of mass-produced sensibility where tastes are marketed and 'products' are developed as a response to a lowest-common-denominator mentality. The search for enlightenment and fulfilment that the arts offer is trampled over by the prevalence of dubiously-named 'talent shows' and reality-television series that document wealthy and superficial lifestyles. The artistic criticism of capitalism is based on a concern that presenting people with mediocre products will render them stupid and unable to engage with the changes going on in their world. Finally, Chiapello notes a newly emergent criticism of capitalism that has been in ascendance since the 1970s: an *ecological* criticism.

Although the most recent shock to the capitalist system was occasioned by the global financial crisis, awareness of the absence of a sustainable global financial system also grew at the same time that concerns accelerated about the emerging ecological crisis and the rise of extremist political movements and worsening social issues. Eve Chiapello sees the potential for three possible responses to the current crisis of capitalism.

The first of these is the potential for developing green capitalism and corporate social responsibility, which will involve continued economic accumulation through technological solutions to the ecological challenge, and a renewed search for alternative technologies and financial investment in research. Another alternative is developing local economies on a human scale. This may involve 'slowing down' the pace of globalisation and creating stronger roles for local governments. The final solution may involve a return to a strong state to manage social and ecological issues.

There has been a global 'turn' to an ecological awareness across the globe. The then-leader of the strongest economic superpower in the world, President Barack Obama, made the environment central to his second inaugural address in January 2013. The first formal statement from Pope Francis I (the leader of the largest organised religion, the largest membership-based organisation and the most enduring organisation in human history) in 2015 was based on the need to address climate change and take responsibility for our 'common home': planet Earth. Theorists have begun to conceptualise how this phenomenon has begun to influence the emergence of a new spirit of capitalism.

Just before the global economy crashed in 2008, many scholars of religion had begun to express a concern that the third spirit of capitalism, which sought to capture the counter-culture's desire for new ways of expressing oneself through work, had begun to degenerate into a corporatised version of narcissism (Carrette & King, 2005; Heelas, 2008). Bell, Taylor & Driscoll (2012) suggested that a more recent spirit of capitalism had begun to emerge, which demonstrated a new level of concern for the natural world or greater levels of economic and social sustainability. British academics Chris Land and Scott Taylor (2010, 2014) conducted fieldwork in organisations and sustainability-oriented events and noticed a newer spirit of capitalism amongst entrepreneurs who sought out a 'middle way' for satisfying the needs of planet and profit. One of the first manifestations of this can be found in what is becoming known as 'eco-preneurship' (as opposed to 'entrepreneurship') in the form of corporate activities and new organisational roles and functions (Wright *et al*, 2012; Phillips, 2013).

This new ethic of capitalism is contested and emergent, and it remains to be seen how it will develop over time. The natural world and new ways of being in the workplace will doubtlessly impact the way that work is done in the future, which will impact on people entering the workforce for the first time, as well as those who seek new work opportunities. This leads us to an area in which all individuals are ethically engaged (whether they believe so or not): the ethics of occupational choice. So the next chapter looks at the area of how individuals choose occupations and enter the world of organised labour.

3: PERSPECTIVES ON ETHICS: EMPLOYEES & EMPLOYMENT

This chapter is concerned with the ethics of work in contemporary organisational life. To understand this, we need to first look at how work in today's *post-industrial* context has undergone significant change in a relatively short period of time and consider the implications of this change for the contemporary workplace. The chapter then turns to the first big business decision faced by most people when leaving education: what work will I do; what profession will I pursue? At first, this may not appear to be related to ethics, but the final section of the chapter (on ethical work choices) demonstrates how it is has become central to the question of how to live an ethical life.

THE ETHICS OF WORK IN THE POST-INDUSTRIAL WORKPLACE

The way we work, organise labour and manage changed very quickly in our recent history. In pre-industrial, pre-modern eras people worked closely with the natural world. Work was integrated into the lived existences of families and small collectives and was primarily concerned with the need to live and survive. This changed from the late-18th century with the onset of the Industrial Revolution. The introduction of new units of production and systems of mass manufacturing resulted in many social changes. While farmers worked together to ensure that food was produced in a sustained way, regardless of the age or gender of the worker, industrialisation introduced a division of labour based on machines, rather than human needs. Because the industrial division of labour was focused on machines, new professions such as mechanical engineering emerged. The principles of mechanical engineering in turn influenced classical and scientific management theory.

Family life became separate to working life. Gradually, this meant that children were removed from the workplace and minimum levels of education for children were brought into law. As children were now *outside* the workplace, a *domestic division of labour* emerged, which meant that women who were mothers were less involved in paid labour as they became responsible for work undertaken in the family sphere (such as childminding and domestic duties). As the factory (rather than the family) became the key unit by which work was organised in the industrial era, it had several other far-reaching effects on the way that people lived and worked.

Edgell (2006) points out that it has often been proposed that James Watt's steam engine is an insufficient symbol for the industrial age; the factory 'clock' has been proposed as a much more appropriate image to associate with the emergence of the factory as a prime location for work. Prior to the factory becoming the centre of how work was organised, work patterns were irregular and were completed according to the passage of the seasons. New time technologies were used to organise a permanent routine that focused on minimising variations and keeping production consistent. The patterns of everyday family life were changed by the preponderance of the 'clock' in industrial management.

As greater levels of education were required to engage with the technical division of labour, the industrial age was accompanied by an expansion in education in general. Prior to this, education was generally pursued only by wealthier members of the elite and tended to focus on 'liberal' or general principles. During the Industrial Revolution, restrictions were gradually placed on the number of hours that children could work, and education began to be publicly funded from the 1830s before becoming compulsory near the end of the 19th century. This meant that workers were more likely to be recruited on the basis of formal   accreditation   and   qualifications,   replacing   previous arrangements where certain families and groups were specialists in particular skills.

The Industrial Revolution also heralded the emergence of modern market economies. In pre-industrial work, families made or repaired things to be used, while in the industrial era items were produced to be sold. Traditional crafts were then superseded by new market offerings that did not focus on serving the family/household unit of production. The modern age made it very difficult for people to earn a living outside the payment of wages in a business enterprise. Pre-industrial societies focused on providing people with a livelihood rather than on money, so workers were often paid in kind or with goods. In pre-industrial societies, the purpose of work was to provide the essentials of life: people worked so they could live. Under industrial capitalism, this changed and the central rationale for work and enterprise became the pursuit of profit.

Industrialisation saw work becoming placed in an institution (a factory, an office, etc.) that was *separate* from everyday life. For Marx, this resulted in workers becoming *alienated* from their true human selves (species alienation), their work (activity alienation), the products they produced (product alienation) and each other (social alienation). Blauner (1964) proposed that it was unfair to assume that all workers suffered from alienation in the same way, and that different types of technological environments would produce different types and levels of alienation. Craft technology environments (which used simple hand-operated machines) would be very different, then, to assembly-line environments that used conveyor belt technology with limited tasks. Machine-tending technological environments (such as those evident in the textile industry) might produce high levels of meaninglessness, powerlessness and self-estrangement, but as social isolation was less a factor in these environments (when compared with assembly-line environments) the type of alienation experienced would be considerably less. Blauner posited that continuous process technology environments (such as that experienced by chemical workers) was low on all the elements of alienation, and could not be considered as alienating as working with assembly line technology.

Braverman (1974) claimed that, as technology becomes more prevalent and embedded in the workplace, workers become less 'skilled' at doing their job. Technology, then, is not neutral, and serves ultimately serves the needs of capitalism. The more sophisticated technology becomes, the less workers 'need' to know about work itself. This means that increases in workplace automation ultimately leads to workers becoming increasingly alienated. Bell (1974) countered this by positing that, following the end of World War II, Western society changed to emphasise service-based non-manufacturing industries. The change from a production-based *industrial society* to a services-based *post-industrial society* pre-empted a fundamental change in how people work and earn. In *post-industrial society*, the possession of private property is less a source of power than the possession of knowledge. The possession of, or ability to generate, knowledge is the key factor of production in post-industrial society.

The recent global recession has drawn attention to the ways in which forms of employment have changed over the post-industrial era which privileges certain forms of work over others. Standing (2011) has drawn attention to how the rules of the world of the industrial citizenship (established in developed economies after World War II) have fundamentally changed over recent years. Industrial citizenship, according to Standing, had offered the industrial proletariat seven forms of security: full, adequately paid employment (labour market security); protection of work contracts and 'tenure' (employment security); opportunities to develop specialisms or become eligible for promotion (job security); a safe workplace (work security); opportunities to become skilled, and to develop these skills, through training (skill reproduction security); fair, 'liveable' payment (income security); opportunities to have workplace concerns addressed through collective action and trade unions (representation security).

Standing claims that the absence of one or more of these rights has contributed to the development of seven new social classes: the Elite; the Salariat; Proficians; the old working class; the Precariat; the unemployed; and the 'dregs'. The Precariat comprise a new social class made up of workers with little employment security or stability (unlike the 'old working class') and little sense of occupational identity or trajectory. Because they work in flexible employment, they are denied many rights usually granted with industrial citizenship, and thus Standing names them *denizens* (or *citizens with partial rights*), rather than full *citizens*. Organisational theorists have done little so far to engage with the Precariat, but Standing claims that political groupings can appeal to the needs of this new class by providing security and representation. A major concern for organisations and managers (and, in particular, human resource professionals and managers) is how to create work systems that address the precariousness of new employment contracts.

THE ETHICS OF OCCUPATIONAL CHOICE

Students reaching the end of their academic careers find themselves on the cusp of making a crucial decision that will undoubtedly impact on their future lives. As all business decisions are, at heart, ethical decisions, it perhaps goes without saying that the decision of which occupation students might pursue is, generally speaking, one of the first ethical business decisions that many make – and one that will have far-reaching implications for a number of years to come.

Surprisingly, it is also a decision that many people do not really give enough consideration to. Our choices about the type of work that we want to do, and the reasons we give ourselves for not pursuing these, demonstrate much about the ethics of how we decide to live our lives. The nature of these decisions, and how people 'end up' doing work that they do not necessarily like or feel 'called' to do, was explored in relation to Gottfredson's theory of occupational choice (1981). Gottfredson found occupational choice to involve the reconciliation of one's self-concept (public and private self) with characteristics of various occupations perceived as options in one's cognitive map of the world of work. This is primarily influenced by other images of personalities of people employed in occupations, the work they do, the lives they live, the rewards they receive and the conditions under which they work.

We start off by eliminating occupational alternatives that conflict with our own self-concept and do not consider these any more through a process known as 'circumscription'. For example, if the idea of working outdoors in many different environments appeals to us, we might avoid occupations that we believe to involve sedentary office work. When we have completed circumscribing our occupational choices, we are left with what Gottfredson calls a 'zone of acceptable alternatives'. At the top of our list in this zone is a small number of aspirant choices (or our most favoured occupational options). However, we may feel that these aspirant choices require a huge amount of time and energy and could be too difficult to attain. They may also require a significant degree of risk; we may fear that investing resources in pursuing our aspirant choices may not eventually bear fruit and will leave us in position where we are frustrated, disappointed or humiliated. This is why we develop a second tier of occupational options in our zone of acceptable alternatives, which Gottfredson refers to as 'realistic choices'. These are occupations that we view as somewhat less desirable than our ideal aspirant choices but we continue to consider them because they are acceptable and accessible. This compromise involves us examining the occupational choices we wish to pursue, and seeking a balance between our fears and energies.

This may make sense at a time when employment opportunities are rare, but it does not mean that it is ethical. Immanuel Kant wrote of ethics involving *a perfect duty to ourselves and others*. Basing our occupational choices on employment that is available may appear commonsense, but instinctively we are aware that, by not pursuing what it is we are meant to do in the long run, we are depriving others of our dedicated service. Why then might people allow this to happen?

Forsyth (1980) suggests that we can hold positions that also vary in intensity. He posits that most individuals can describe their personal ethical positions by considering where they stand in relation to two separate axes:

o **Relativism:** which involves the degree to which individuals reject beliefs about the existence of universal moral standards;

o **Idealism:** which asserts that there are universal moral standards and that all people should follow them.

If we consider these axes as poles that individuals identify with at a strong or weak level, then a greater variety of ethical positions are produced.

People who have both strong relativism and idealism are *situationists*, who reject universal moral rules and prefer to analyse the ethics of each action or thing on the basis of the circumstances in which they are performed. Situationists might think about the best thing to do when faced with a moral dilemma in terms of the events and individuals involved rather than any other moral framework. Situationists are primarily concerned with the context in which ethics are done.

People who have strong relativism and low idealism are *subjectivists*, who base their judgements on whether something is ethical on personal values rather than universal moral principles. A subjectivist would view an ethically complicated situation through the lens of their own personal experiences and values, and analyse it according to what they believe they would do if they had found themselves in the same situation as the people involved. Subjectivists are mainly concerned with doing ethics through the prism of their own implicit ethical framework or self.

People who have low relativism and high idealism are *absolutists*, who are guided by a firm belief in universal moral standards and assume that the best possible outcome can always be achieved by following these. Absolutists would apply a set of moral rules that they believe should apply to everyone; a set of rules that they believe to be based on universal absolute truths.

People who have low affiliations for both idealism and relativism are *exceptionalists* who are guided by moral absolutes to a certain degree, but remain pragmatically open to exceptions to these standards. Exceptionalists might view an ethical situation through the lens of universal moral rules, but would also be conscious of how the social circumstances and business culture at a particular point in time might have obscured the judgement of the key parties involved in this ethical scenario.

Exceptionalism provides us with an insight into one of the most dominant ethical paradigms evidenced in the world today: *utilitarianism*. Utilitarianism can be considered exceptionalist because it asserts that certain moral standards are true ('the greatest good for the greatest number should always be sought out'), but it also recognises that certain standards need to be understood in more detail in order to prescribe ethical responses that are appropriate to specific circumstances.

VOCATIONAL IDEATION & ETHICAL OCCUPATIONAL CHOICES

Central to Weber's concept of the Protestant work ethic (discussed in **Chapter 2**) was that of the *vocation* or *calling*. Giddens (1992) writes that Weber's concept of the calling, as it was found in the Protestant work ethic, projected religion into everyday working life as an obligation on the individual to fulfil their duties.

The establishment of this moral imperative became fundamental to how capitalism was enculturated. The calling, for Weber, was a personal obligation for individuals to ensure whatever work they did was meaningful, because it indicated that it was divinely ordained for them by God. For the believer, work was no longer something one did solely for payment, but 'a life task, a definite field in which to work' (Weber *et al*, 1992: 39). By subjecting themselves entirely to God's will, the faithful were called to commit themselves to the occupation in which they found themselves.

Regardless of the *external* reasons why people might choose a particular occupation field (employability, stability and remuneration, etc.), the *internal* reasons have a greater degree of salience in relation to vocations. In *Science as Vocation*, Weber (1919) discusses vocation as a commitment to a specialist area of work that the individual engages with in terms that almost equate with religious zeal. It is important to remember that Weber talks of scientists who have discovered their vocation as being committed to (or even obsessed by) their work, rather than their career: their vocation manifests itself in *what* they do, rather than the rewards that they get from it.

There has been a resurgence of interest in the concept of vocation in recent years. A vocation is something that nourishes the person's whole life (including their non-work life), but working in a vocational field without having a calling will produce negative results in other parts of the person's life. In this sense, finding out which work we will do is perhaps one of the most important ethical decisions that any individual can make. Many begin on an occupational path that they believe themselves to be suitable for, but either end up becoming disconnected or disengaged from it. Others, when they realise that they have begun something that they are not suited to, seek out ways to find which direction they should commit to instead. For most, though, discovering which path we should pursue is complicated by factors that lie outside ourselves.

There are a number of reasons why individuals find it difficult to think about their vocation, but easier to think about careers. The 'career' has become the dominant paradigm for how we think about work in contemporary society. We talk of professional footballers, musicians and actors having careers, and use this as a way of determining how well they are performing, usually in relation to their popularity. Careers are visible representations of work effectiveness, but they tell us nothing about the reasons why people are successful. The prevalence of the career discourse continues to dominate how we advise people to make decisions about their education and their working life (Cullen, 2011b).

Vocational ideation (Cullen, 2013) is a process of identifying, examining and developing an understanding of one's calling. A new development in career planning and thinking about ethical work choices, vocational ideation provides a structure by which individuals can go against the dominant *career* narrative and actively test the field of work in which they can fulfil themselves intellectually, ethically and socially. It involves deeply engaging with the idea that everyone is being *called*. If a person is not religious, this calling can come from a person's interests or talents, a sector or an organisation. Pursuing a job involves seeking out money; the search for a career involves seeking economic value and career advancement; pursing a calling is how we find work that creates monetary and personal value for ourselves *and* for other people. This does not mean that one need work only in social enterprises or ethically-oriented organisations; individuals who work in commercial organisations, and who are pursuing their vocations, benefit their clients and society at large by working in ways that serve not only the needs of their organisations, but also by doing things in the most ethical way possible.

Vocational ideation is actually a menu of practices that are undertaken at three distinct stages. *Vocational pre-ideation* involves individuals considering the amount of energy and types of activities that they currently engage in. The individual is then asked to draft a working statement on the type of work that they would ideally like to pursue and what they think they would like to *get* from this process. The next stage of the process is *vocational ideation research,* where individuals actively think about and critically interrogate the reasons for why they want to pursue a particular calling. A critical part of this stage involves the individual 'trying on' the most unappealing part of the role so they can get the clearest picture of the challenges that are involves in it.

Developing a critical perspective on one's ideated vocation is crucial because people who have strong work ethics or vocations have always been open to exploitation. Weber outlines this early in *The Protestant Ethic & The Spirit of Capitalism,* where he draws attention to capitalism as a system that requires low wages to be paid. Because workers will naturally resist this: 'Labour must, on the contrary be performed as if it were an absolute end in itself, a calling' (1992: 25).

In a highly controversial article in the *Journal of Health Economics* in 2005, Heyes suggested that proposals to increase the pay of nurses, as a measure to address the shortage of numbers entering the nursing profession, would result in attracting the 'wrong sort'. By 'wrong sort', he meant people who are only interested in the stability, mobility and money that the nursing profession can provide. His logic goes as follows: if nurses were paid more, the profession would become full of individuals who would do it for reasons other than patient care, and this would eventually impact on the quality of care provided.

The final stage is concerned with *vocational post-ideation reflection.* This is conducted at the stage when an individual has completed their pre-ideation and vocational research and involves comparing their expectations of the work with the lived reality of it. Even if the result has been negative, if the individual deals with the disappointment of finding out that the work they thought they wanted to do bears no relation to what it practically involves, they have learned important things about their own work-orientation that can help them begin the process again from a more honest, ethical position.

Through this chapter so far, we've examined some of the ways in which work and its meaning has changed since the advent of the industrial revolution. We've also looked at some of the models that have been used to assist people make ethical decisions about the type of work that they do or would like to do by exploring Gottfredson's theory of occupational choice (1981) or the vocational ideation process (Cullen, 2013). However, while both of these processes demonstrate the social nature of making career decisions, neither addresses the situation where individuals may simply have no idea about the work they are best suited for or should do. Even when people are set on a career path that they have chosen and dedicated significant amounts of time and personal resources to pursuing, they may still be unsure whether they are doing the right thing with their life. René Girard's (1966) theory of mimetic desire may provide some interesting context in this regard. To understand mimetic desire, however, we first need to understand *mimesis*.

Mimesis & Mimetic Desire

Human beings have lived in social and political configurations that we have come to know as 'civilizations' for around 6,000 years. The civilization that emerged in 4th and 5th century Greece maintains an enduring influence on how people live their lives in contemporary society. For example, the concept of democracy is often thought to have emerged around this time in the city-state of Athens, which had become a centre of artistic, educational, political and intellectual life. One of the main figures involved in the foundation of ethical thought was the philosopher Plato (who lived from the late 5th to the mid-4th century BCE), who established the prototype for what would become the university in his school which was known as 'The Academy'. Like many of the philosophers of this era, Plato made contributions to a variety fields. For example, his book *The Republic* is a discussion of how society should be ordered, the development of the people within in it, leadership, justice, etc. It is perhaps one of the earliest examples of the understanding that our character informs, and is informed by, the social structures in which we find ourselves.

One of the most commonly-known of Plato's many ideas is his *Theory of Forms*. Plato believed that the world we experience is merely a reflection of some greater reality that is beyond our comprehension as human beings. In *The Republic*, Plato used an allegory of prisoners chained in a cave, who know no other reality, to illustrate this. In the cave, the prisoners see shadows on the wall from the sun outside and they assume that this is reality. The implication is that, as human beings, we are not capable of really understanding the true nature of ourselves and the universe. It is probably easy to see the huge influence that Platonic thinking had on the intellectual development of monotheistic religion.

Plato had a long-held aversion to poetry and its place in Athenian society. Janko (1987) points out that poetry in Ancient Greece was the equivalent of today's mass media. It would be memorised, performed and discussed and was the main form of entertainment in that society. Plato had many objections to the poetry of his time, as he believed that it was composed and consumed under the influence of emotion (as opposed to reason), and that poets teach things that they do not have direct experience about and represent sacred entities as imperfect. All of these would impede the chances of achieving the perfect republic. Another of Plato's significant objections to poetry is that it is highly *mimetic*.

Because Plato believed that we can only apprehend real truth by intellectual investigation, he felt that poetry was only able to represent genuine reality in a way that is two steps away from its real nature. Plato believed that our immortal souls know the true forms of things before we were born into human form. We know, for example, what love is. Then, in our human form, when we believe we fall in love with someone, we are trying, imperfectly, to recall what that true form of love is. A contemporary love song, then, is written in a way that is one step away from the real transcendental nature of love and our personal experience of love, because it is written and recorded in a studio far away from us for commercial gain. It has nothing to do with our personal experience at a human or transcendental level. Poetry (or art), according to Plato, is dishonest or harmful because it *imitates* true reality at a number of removes. The Greek word *mimesis* means imitation.

Plato's student and intellectual successor, Aristotle (384-322), greatly advanced the concept of mimesis while challenging Plato's aversion to the arts of his time. Aristotle rejected Plato's theory of forms and the idea that this world is a pale reflection of a greater transcendent reality. Instead, he asserted the value of studying and understanding the world as we humans actually perceive and experience it. He advocated that we analyse the natural phenomena that we perceive with our senses and then apply our findings to the study of philosophy. Aristotle, then, with his interest in the world and perceptions and beliefs of 'ordinary' people is less of an elitist and idealist than Plato. We can see the differences between these two approaches in the famous 'School of Athens' fresco by Raphael, where many figures from the world of ancient science, poetry and philosophy are represented. At the centre of this painting are Plato and Aristotle. Plato points up at the heavens; perhaps demonstrating that he believed that life on earth is dictated by a transcendent realm that we cannot comprehend. Aristotle gestures downwards, which could be taken to signify that we best understand life and how to live it by developing a detailed, accurate understanding of the world and our place in it.

Aristotle agreed with Plato that poetry is mimetic, but in a different way. Janko (1987) points out that the ancient Greeks did not distinguish between imitation, copying and representation in how they used and applied the term *mimesis*. Plato saw poetry as a (poor) *imitation* of a reality that we cannot understand. Aristotle saw art and poetry as a *re-presentation* of life and reality.

Because art represents (or is a *re-presentation* of) reality according to Aristotle, it can help us understand reality in new ways and clarify the true nature and purpose (or *telos*) of things. It can also help us raise our level of consciousness of things that we may not have been conscious of beforehand. The emotional nature of poetry, therefore, can help us understand the emotional forces that contribute to our ethical life. Where Plato saw emotions to be irrational forces that should be supressed in order to develop a rational mindset, Aristotle saw them as key components in helping us learn how to react to the world around us in an appropriate way. This appropriate response is a central idea in Aristotle's ethics. Through mimesis, art can assist us to form good character and settled dispositions.

So what does the idea of mimesis, or imitation, have to do with the difficulties people might experience in relation to making a choice about their future occupational path? René Girard's theory of mimetic desire has many implications for the ethics of leadership and organisational life, but has been successfully applied in helping people to make decisions about their future work. Girard was originally a French historian who began his studies in Paris when it was occupied during World War II. Following the war, he left France to complete PhD studies in the US and began teaching French. He was very soon given European literature classes to teach, and had to deliver a course on European Novelists. The problem was that Girard had not read all of these works! He would later state that, for much of the time, he was 'just a few pages ahead of the students' in completing his reading of the texts before delivering classes to the students (Cayley, 2001). He decided to examine what made these 'great' novels similar (rather than outstanding) and in doing so, he developed his theory of mimetic desire which was first published in English as *Deceit, Desire & the Novel* in the 1960s and has increasingly been applied to understanding conflict in a variety of social and organisational settings.

Girard proposed that what made certain novels great is that they all expose what he called 'the romantic lie', which is the notion that our desires emanate from a creative inner depth. For example, the idea that one day we will have an epiphany and discover the true meaning and purpose of our lives. Girard challenged this and said that, in truth, we are very uncertain about what it is we want from life. We decide that we desire certain things only because we see other people desiring them. In other words, we borrow our desires from other people. We desire things not because they are inherently desirable to us, but because another person's desire for them has made them appealing to us.

We may have instinctual urges, but these are often coloured by what we see other people desiring in fulfilling their instincts. This idea runs counter to many motivational theorists, such as Maslow, whose hierarchy of needs model proposes that, once we satisfy an internal physical, social, ego-related or self-actualising desire, our motivations are recalibrated to reaching our next level of fulfilment. Desire, according to Girard, is 'triangular', in that to truly desire something we need to see somebody else desiring it also. Thus, desire is mediated by another person.

However, the fact that we need another party to configure our desires means that they can become potential rivals. Have you ever wondered why people you were previously close to suddenly became antagonistic towards you? Could they have perceived you achieving or desiring something that they themselves unconsciously desire? This is what Girard named *mimetic rivalry* and it explains why people or groups who share the greatest number of similarities often have the most intense and enduring conflicts. The closer we are to somebody else, the greater the possibility of mimesis and the more likely you will share the same goals. The great tragedy of mimetic rivalry is that it can be sustained long after the initial object of desire has ceased to exist. Groups or individuals who undergo such high levels of rivalry often mimetically copy their actions against each other, ironically becoming more like their rival as a result of their mimetic rivalry.

We will return to Girard's theory of mimetic desire as we examine culture and leadership in later chapters, but for now we consider how this impacts on the area of occupational choice. Perhaps one of the best examples of this is Peter Thiel, who is best known for his central role in co-founding PayPal and financing Facebook. Thiel did a BA in philosophy at Stanford (where Girard taught), before proceeding to study law (also at Stanford). Thiel has discussed in many fora how he competed with other law graduates for a position in a prestigious law firm. However, he left this coveted job after one year as it failed to fulfil him (and did not appear to fulfil more senior people in the firm). The theory of mimetic desire demonstrated to him that he desired the role in the law firm because others desired it and competed for it; not because he wanted it himself. When he decided to leave, some colleagues joked that they didn't know if it was possible to do so. Thiel instead sought out investment and entrepreneurial activities where there was a real need, but not necessarily where others were already active, as this would only result in diverting energy into mimetic rivalry and conflict.

Understanding Girard's theories of mimetic desire and rivalry allows us to look under the surface of our conscious career plans (or lack of them) and asks us how we can go about creating real value in unique and original ways that are free from the cultures and systems that have been constructed and created for us to exist in. Part of understanding how we might do this involves understanding these organisational configurations and how they emerge. We turn to this in our study of organisational life in the next chapter.

4: Perspectives on Ethics: Organisational Life

Chapter 3 examined the ethics of work from the perspective of the person who is preparing to enter the workforce. This chapter examines what this person can expect when they actually begin working. One of the great 'silences' that exists in organisational theory is what actually happens when individuals first encounter the workplaces that they have trained, sacrificed and strived to enter.

Organisations, like any other large or small social grouping, develop behavioural norms, power structures and traditions that act like signposts for what the organisation's members believe can and cannot be said or done within the workplace. As these are anchored in a shared set of inter-subjective behaviours, the people in the organisation who are responsible for ensuring that these cultural norms 'happen' are often unaware that they are doing so. Because of this, organisational newcomers often make cultural errors in saying the 'wrong thing' to a person in a position of unofficial power, dressing in a way that violates an established (but unwritten) code, or representing themselves in a manner that does not meet the presentational norms of the firm. More importantly, it is difficult for current members of the organisation to assist newcomers understand what these norms are because they themselves are unlikely to be aware of what they are. This chapter explores the ethical dimensions of such norms by examining the way that culture and structure can impact on how employees and managers participate in organisational life.

CULTURE & ETHICS

Culture is one of the most 'theorised' topics in the entire field of organisational studies, and there are many definitions of what culture is and how it 'works' on employees in organisations. Throughout the history of anthropology (the study of humans), there have been multiple definitions of culture (Kroeber & Kluckhohn, 1952; Geertz, 1973), but many see morality as a core dimension (Kluckhohn & Strodtbeck, 1973). As mentioned earlier, Freud saw cultural forces as moral strictures that individuals *internalise* in order to control instincts that would otherwise lead to the annihilation of the group. In *The Future of an Illusion: Civilisation & Its Discontents & Other Works* (1930/2001) he writes that the main way in which this is done is through the unpleasant emotion of guilt. Because being guilty is such a painful experience, individuals will avoid doing anything that will cause it to emerge in themselves. But why do some people feel guilty about doing certain things and not about other things?

Freud writes that this has to do with our development as infants. As helpless individuals, we rely on others (primarily parent-figures) to ensure our survival by providing for us and protecting us from danger. We come to understand at an early stage of our lives that they do this because of love, and we return this love in turn. Freud theorised that the sense of guilt is fear that somebody who we genuinely love will remove their love from us. As we develop psychologically, this fear of the loss of love extends to society, and is reinforced in our psyche by the superego.

Freud did not discuss 'culture' *per se*, but rather 'civilisation'. He was writing about his own cultural experiences at a particular point in time and cultural psychologists, such as Shweder (1991), have demonstrated that what would be a cause of a deep sense of guilt in some cultures are not problematic in others. This is also true of many understandings of organisational culture, which discuss it as shared systems of meaning amongst members of an organisation (or groups within an organisation) that delineate certain behaviours as moral and others as immoral (Watson, 2001). Culture is important for anyone who is interested in studying organisational life, because it examines how we develop *shared* understandings of certain things. As such, disciplines such as anthropology, sociology and psychoanalysis are useful to us in examining ethics. Indeed, the word 'ethics' is obtained from the Greek word *ethos*, which is strongly related to culture. One of the leading cultural anthropologists, Clifford Geertz, wrote that the ethos of a group:

> ... is the tone, character, and quality of their life, its moral and aesthetic stuff and mood; it is the underlying attitude towards themselves and their world that life reflects. (1973: 127)

Thus, we are *doing* ethics when we think about the 'taken-for-granted' way in which we experience organisations or social groups.

There is a strong tradition of examining the ethics of the 'everyday' in cultural anthropology. American anthropologist Nancy Scheper-Hughes has long demonstrated how 'everyday violence' is committed within cultural groups against their own members in order to maintain a particular social order that facilitates the group's sustainability. In her study of a rural Irish community, *Saints, Scholars & Schizophrenics* (1979), she demonstrates how families gently communicated a message to certain members that they are somehow less 'able' for the outside world. This ensure that they remain at home to look after farms, while their siblings leave to travel, pursue careers and start relationships and families of their own. The loneliness and isolation experienced by these unfortunate individuals often results in mental health problems. In a later book, *Death Without Weeping* (1992), she discusses how mothers living in dire poverty in a South American *favela* use cultural norms to hasten the deaths of weaker, more sickly children. Culture may sustain certain norms and groups, but we are naive if we imagine that there is never a cost for another group in such situations.

These are two examples of how encountering the everyday can change our understanding, not just of how human beings behave under pressurised or threatening circumstances, but of how we can use a cultural lens to understand how ethical norms are reconfigured by culture. Although culture is perhaps one of the most interesting ways in which we can explore organisational life, it is important to remember that it is also one of the most contested fields in organisational studies.

Just as there are many ways in which researchers understand culture (Geertz, 1973; Smircich, 1983), there are significant differences between the ways in which organisational theorists look at the culture of work and organisations. Some theorists (for example, Hofstede, 2001; Trompenaars & Hampden-Turner, 2012) have proposed that it is possible to discern the difference between national business cultures, and although these models are still very much in use they have been criticised on the grounds they are based mainly on ethnocentric survey data and do not capture the important nuances of how people in various cultures actually live their lives. In an article published in the *Leadership & Organisation Development Journal* in 2004, I reported research on different forms of management cultures that could be found in the public, private and not-for-profit sectors in Ireland. Leadership and commercial acumen were highly valued in the private sector; public sector managers were expected to be strong networkers across a variety of organisations; and managers in the not-for-profit sector were expected to be entrepreneurial self-initiators.

When we focus on the field of organisational culture, there are also many ways in which it can be studied (Morgan, 1986; Alvesson, 2002), but it might be posited that there are essentially two main approaches: the first is *managed* approaches to organisational cultures, and the second is *process-based* approaches. It is important to consider the ethical implications of each set of approaches.

ORGANISATIONAL CULTURE: MANAGED APPROACHES

The first group (*managed approaches*) proposed that organisational cultures are things that organisations possess (Parker, 2000; Smircich, 1983), which can change or influence to improve their strategic positions. This, of course, assumes that culture is relatively unchanging and is shared by every member of the organisation. Such approaches became popular in the early 1980s when Tom Peters and Robert Waterman published *In Search of Excellence* (1984), which became an international bestseller and made Peters one of the best-known management gurus in the world at the time. Peters and Waterman's text spoke to concerns that the US was in danger of losing its position as the global economic superpower due to a lack of productivity, innovation and work ethics in many traditional industries. Peters compared these to the work cultures of Japanese organisations, where workers valued their organisations in ways that created 'strong' cultures where individual gain was less of a priority than the success of the organisation. Culture, in other words, is key to performance. The success of *In Search of Excellence* resulted in a mini-publishing boom of books with advice on how managers can change their cultures and become competitive again.

Many of these early books on organisational culture attempted to help managers understand their cultures and several offered classification systems, such as Deal & Kennedy's 'tough guy/macho', 'work hard/play hard', 'bet your company' and 'process' cultures (1982) and Miles & Snow's 'defender', 'prospector', 'analyser' and 'reactor' cultures (1978). One of the most famous typologies is Charles Handy's (1993), which proposed that there are four main types of organisational culture: *power* cultures that have centralised decision-making systems (represented by the ancient Greek god Zeus, or a web); *role* cultures where different sources of knowledge or action required or produced by the organisation are placed into various bureaucratic pillars that support a management pediment (represented by Apollo, or a temple); *task* cultures in large complex organisations where power is distributed throughout the organisation and tasks are best accomplished at nodal points of this network (represented by Athena or a matrix); and *cluster* cultures that are made up of loose affiliations of individuals who work together for mutual gain (represented by Dionysus, who Handy associates with self-oriented individuals).

This, however, is not where the story of organisational culture ends. Occasionally, attempts to create 'cultures of performance' have been clearly linked to organisational failure and leader derailment. Culture is not necessarily about what is shared in an organisation, but also refers to what is *not shared*.

Schein (1996), for example, discusses how three sub-cultures can exist in organisations. These three sub-cultures have different referent groups that they seek to make an impression on, and because of this they often fail to communicate, cooperate and learn. These cultures include: the *operator* culture, the *engineer* (or professional) culture, and the *executive* culture. The operator sub-culture consists of the people who do the operational work of the organisation; members of this sub-culture develop norms that ensure the group bonds and polices itself. Members of the professional (or engineering) subculture have been trained and educated outside their organisation and must observe the requirements of their profession. They do this by maintaining membership of their professional organisation. Finally, the CEO and senior managers of the organisation make up an executive sub-culture that is concerned with maintaining the commercial viability of the organisation and communicating this to the broader community.

Joanne Martin (1992) has similarly written that there are three perspectives that can be taken on any organisational culture: *integrated* perspectives are essentially managed views that see the organisational culture as something shared by all members in a consistent way; *differentiated* perspectives take into account the existence of sub-cultures within organisations which all present different perspectives on the organisational culture; and *fragmented* perspectives address confusion and lack of clarity about an organisation's proclaimed values, which an integrated perspective assumes are consistently held by all members. Essentially, fragmented perspectives open up the possibility of there being multiple-points of view on the culture of an organisation. My own research on a culture change initiative in a large Irish services organisation (Cullen, 2011b) found that there is never one singular response to an organisational change but that responses differ depending on the social, cultural and religious background of the individual.

None of the above should be taken to infer that managed cultures to organisational culture are of no value at all. Managed approaches to culture are often critical when understanding how to make necessary change when the culture of the organisation is resistant to it, and when trying to establish improved standards in the organisation. Two examples of this, which are briefly outlined below, are Deming's TQM and Johnson's Culture Web.

Operations used to be perceived as primarily concerned with production and distribution; more recently, operations has aligned more closely with the discipline of marketing in order to engage a variety of stakeholders to work closely together to provide enhanced value to customers. The work of W. Edwards Deming in his pioneering of the principles of total quality management (TQM) was fundamental to this change. Deming was a key advisor to Japan in the aftermath of World War II and helped address fears about the quality of Japanese products and services that were seen as impeding economic development. Deming advocated building quality into products from the outset and striving for continuous improvement through reducing variations in quality. The principles of TQM quickly became of interest to companies outside Japan. From an ethical perspective, Deming's advocacy of quality equated to a reduction in costs and waste over time. If companies focused on reducing costs alone, this would mean that quality would decrease, and costs associated with decreased quality would gradually increase. By broadening the focus of operations to all stakeholders concerned with delivering value to customers, Deming stressed the importance of collaborative values such as employee empowerment, team-based approaches to work and increased co-operation with suppliers. A large part of the drive for quality stressed the human and social elements of organisational life as being instrumental to the creation of customer satisfaction. Focusing on quality, and the team structure required to deliver it, results in profound cultural change.

One of the most globally prominent strategy theorists is Gerry Johnson, and in 1992 he published a hugely influential model for demonstrating the relationship between culture and strategic change. By the early-1990s, much of the initial hype about culture change and strategic planning was beginning to be questioned by both academics and managers. Was it possible to genuinely change an organisation's culture, particularly when there was so much resistance amongst staff and line managers? What was the point of spending large amounts of money on strategic planning and consultancy, when the results were questionable? Culture and strategy did not seem to get on very well together!

Johnson used the term 'paradigm' rather than 'culture', as it best represented the unique perspective of managers and employees who worked in unique organisational cultures (rather than ones typified by classification systems). These cultures all had unique histories and belief systems, but these often obscured the reality of life and markets outside the organisation for its members. The organisational paradigm only allows its members to see the organisation in a particular way, which means that it cannot observe how its operating environment is changing. New technologies, disruptive innovations, customer tastes, economic circumstances, social values etc., all change what the market expects from the organisation at a pace that exceeds the organisation's ability to change. Over time, this results in a growing distance between the organisation and the market in which it operates; an increasing void that Johnson named 'strategic drift'. Because the paradigm is informed by stories and myths, organisational structures, power structures, rituals and routines, control systems and stories about heroes and villains, these need to be addressed and altered to change the paradigm into one that is bettered suited to the changing environment. The greater the degree of strategic drift, the more radical and urgent these alterations need to be to save the organisation.

Although Deming and Johnson proposed approaches that have been listed here as managed approaches to culture change, they serve as a useful bridge to unmanaged approaches to studying culture. This is because they both realise that every organisational reality has emerged on its own terms over time and has a cultural logic that is local and unique to itself. Organisational cultural scholars who study organisational life from this perspective often apply a group of methods variously known as ethnography, which involve spending large amounts of time within a cultural setting in order to understand how what appears to be ethical, normal behaviour in one workplace would lead to instant dismissal in others.

Organisational Culture as Process

In an ethnographic account of working life in a medical centre that specialised in the treatment of sexually transmitted diseases (2001), the medical anthropologist Melissa Parker describes encountering a number of practices that would likely result in severe repercussions if individuals engaged with them in another setting. Nurses, doctors and administrative staff contributed to a highly sexualised environment through physical contact, flirtatious behaviour and constant banter and joking about sex. At the same time, there was an expectation that staff not be too sensitive towards the feelings of patients and the privacy and anonymity of service users was not prioritised. These norms had not developed, however, as a result of unchecked behaviours that had been allowed to flourish. Rather, they were the responses of individuals to the pressures of working in an environment that dealt with important health issues in a context that most people do not generally encounter. In this environment, patients could present with issues and conditions that they were either deeply embarrassed about or were indifferent to. The overt sexuality and indifference to sensitivity and confidentiality became a form of armour that staff members could put on to protect themselves from the bizarre, traumatic or deeply sad cases that they dealt with on a daily basis.

The idea that people change their emotional responses to something that happens in the workplace was first explored by Arlie Russell Hochschild in her book, *The Managed Heart: Commercialization of Human Feeling* (1983). Hochschild introduced the concept of *emotional labour* to the field of organisational studies and the sociology of the workplace. Organisational behaviourists often focus on examining emotion in the workplace as something that is part of the personality of individual employees, or something that can be altered in relation to the working environment or the management style of supervisors. Instead, Hochschild demonstrated that many workers (particularly in the service industries) had to manipulate how they appeared to be feeling (and, in some cases, had to alter the way in which they actually felt) in order to be successful in a market-based environment. Doing this is not easy: if a member of cabin crew is terrified during severe weather conditions, it requires a huge amount of additional work for them to appear calm and focused so they can assist passengers.

Psychoanalytically-informed ethnographies have been very useful in studying how approaches to changing culture have impacted on employees in an organisation. One particularly useful concept in this regard is the idea of an organisation's *psychostructure*, which is the means by which individuals unconsciously identify with an organisational identity. To understand the process by which individuals come to do this, we first need to understand another psychoanalytical term that has entered everyday discourse: *narcissism*. Often when we hear somebody being discussed as 'narcissistic' or 'a narcissist', it is usually done in a disapproving way, but psychoanalysis considers narcissism as something that is a normal part of psychological development.

Gabriel *et al* (1999) offer an excellent overview of how the developmental experience of narcissism contributes to the development of organisational psychostructures. New-born babies experience life as if they are the centre of the world. When they are hungry, tired or uncomfortable, their cries ensure prompt attention from their mother. As far as they know, the world exists for them; this is the experience of *primary narcissism*. However, this experience is often quickly replaced by a sharp realisation that the world does not exist for them alone and the world becomes experienced as a place that can contain dangerous and hostile forces. In order not to succumb to these forces, the individual needs to develop a sense of self-love through recognising attractive qualities in objects or individuals. This supports the development of what Freud named the *ego-ideal* or the moral perfection that individuals seek to identify themselves with. Failing to live up the very high expectations of our ego-ideal will result in us experiencing *moral anxiety*.

Organisations and its leaders can provide an ego-ideal for individuals. They can gratify the individual's economic needs, but also their need for a meaningful existence. Organisations can present examples of ideal individuals to which we can aspire to be like. *Psychostructure* represents the characteristics or achievements that could make up an individual's ego-ideal and which they believe are found to exist in an organisation, its culture, leaders and employees. Catherine Casey's (1999) ethnography of an organisation applying the team-based principles of TQM found that its psychostructure required employees to develop personal strategies to accommodate the 'family'-like culture of the organisation. Failing to meet the demands of the organisational ego-ideal produced uncertainty, guilt and anxiety for employees, which in turn reinforced narcissistic tendencies.

More recently, anthropologists of the workplace have turned their focus to some of the huge issues that have impacted the world in recent years. Karen Ho's *Liquidated: An Ethnography of Wall Street* (2009) was published following the global financial crash. While many economists had demonstrated why the crash was inevitable, sociologists studied how it impacted on many of the innocent victims of the crash and legal experts discussed who should be punished and how we could stop such things from happening again. As ethicists of the workplace, however, we are interested in why people working in financial institutions continued doing what they did in the face of clear, impending disaster. Ho conducted her fieldwork while working for an investment bank and, through her participation and observation of daily, lived working life in Wall Street, she observed that the employees *internalised* the dominant logic of the market. The Wall Street firms reassured themselves that their actions were 'legitimate' by ensuring that they recruited highly-qualified but inexperienced graduates from elite Ivy League universities. Despite not having management experience, the new recruits found themselves in a position where they could influence the quality of working life for many people in a range of industries. As the financial markets rewarded quick returns on investment, so too did the working environment of Wall Street where investment bankers were aware that they could lose their own jobs at any minute. At the same time, they received huge bonuses for completing successful trades. Working in an environment where individuals could be sacked at any minute meant that they had to secure significant bonuses to cushion the impact of becoming suddenly unemployed. Sustainable, long-term value creation for clients became de-prioritised in favour of the short-term returns provided by, say, the commission received on completing the sale of a sub-prime mortgage. In an environment where the long-term is never part of the culture, it is perhaps understandable how the conditions for a severe crisis emerged from working practices at the centre of the financial world.

Ethnographic accounts of workplace culture can inform us of what has happened in the past, but more importantly, they can also tell us what we can do if we encounter such scenarios in the future. Many people tell of the personal stress that they underwent when either witnessing or reporting ethical violations in the workplace. Few people wish to do wrong or to harm other people, so how can an understanding of culture change work environments where ethical behaviour is at risk of being compromised?

In late January 1986, the Challenger Space Shuttle exploded shortly after take-off. It soon emerged that the manufacturers of a key component of the Space Shuttle had warned that, due to a recent temperature drop, the launch would be highly risky and had issued a 'no fly' recommendation to NASA. In her analysis of the reasons for the decision to launch the Space Shuttle in 1986, despite warnings not to do so, Dianne Vaughan (1996) used a mechanism to demonstrate how the interplay of organisational culture, the broader social structure of a situation and the demands on an individual professional's or manager's agency can lead to such decisions being made. Decisions, then, are made at the point where structure (the broader socio-economic milieu), culture (the way in which the organisation and its members have learned to do things over time and have to come to accept them as normal) and agency (the degree of freedom that individuals have to act independently of structure, rules, institutions, etc.) come together.

The *structural* elements that influenced the Challenger launch decision resulted from President Reagan's drive to reduce public spending. NASA came under pressure to reduce costs, justify spending and self-fund. As a result, much of NASA's work, previously conducted within the organisation, was outsourced. These changes contrasted with the existing managerial *culture* within NASA, where engineers and technicians worked together to resolve existing problems on-site. NASA had always worked on projects that were cutting-edge (such as putting human beings on the moon!), which meant that risk (and deviating from procedures) gradually became normalised. The *agency* of parties was compromised as the sub-contractors often depended on NASA for work and they needed to maintain positive work relationships with the organisation. NASA's agency was also compromised. Fearful that the public was increasingly concerned about costly space missions during a recession and aware of a growing lack of public interest in the space programme, NASA initiated a 'teacher-in-space' project that aimed to rekindle the appeal of space exploration to Americans. The teacher selected for the Challenger mission, Christa McAuliffe, was scheduled to teach lessons from space that would have to be cancelled if the launch was not to proceed as planned.

Although culture can bind people together in positive action, it also has an ability to constrain them and prevent them from acting ethically. The ethnographic accounts summarised above (and mentioned in previous chapters) provide examples of how culture and societal structures and expectations can impact on the unconscious organisational lives of employees and managers and end up compromising their ethics and morals. Elias's civilising process suggests that broader social changes contribute to the development of individual superegos and sense of shame. In the final section of this chapter, we will examine some of the psychodynamic processes that help us understand why and how this happens.

Culture, Ethics & Organisational Life

Before examining some of the theoretical stances on how and why culture influences our ethical selves at a fundamental unconscious level, it is important to recognise that the field of employment law and employee rights have done much to protect organisational members. Culture can be an ethical 'blinder' to people in organisations, which means that the introduction of an organisational newcomer often provides a critical opportunity for reflection on ethical climates and cultures that have emerged in organisations (Cullen, 2008a). Up until recently, newcomers may have been fearful about whistleblowing due to the potential reputational impact that it might have on their future careers, but perhaps more significantly it is important to acknowledge that, when a new staff member joins an organisation, they may simply be unaware of the cultural and structural issues that their managers may have faced. It is unfair to expect new recruits to bear the responsibility for addressing ethical issues that they may observe when they first join an organisation. However, their questions about the morality of certain practices and processes may provide important moments of clarity and reflection for the managers to whom these questions are addressed.

One way in which individuals often exercise ethical agency as a result of their moral identity clashing with their employing organisation's culture is through whistleblowing, which is any group of acts undertaken by employees to expose their employers to an outside agency for perceived ethical violations. Protection for whistleblowers is provided by a series of legal instruments in many countries. In Ireland, it is provided through the *Protected Disclosures Act, 2014*, which protects workers in all sectors who report: criminal offences; breaches of legal obligations; threats to health and safety; miscarriages of justice; improper use of public funds; and attempts to conceal wrongdoing.

People who 'blow the whistle' on such activities are protected from dismissal, penalties from employers, actions for damages and threats to their family and, furthermore, enjoy protection of their identity. The recent introduction of this legislation means that large employers may have to develop policies and establish mechanisms to enable whistleblowing (such as phone lines, review committees, and cultural audits). This important legal innovation is vital to ensure that an individual employee is not forced to compromise their personal values when faced with wrongdoing by the organisational employer. The fact remains that members of organisations who witness such ethical violations often turn a 'blind eye' to them, often at a great personal psychological expense. More interestingly, people who clearly believe that they act with the utmost integrity and honesty can find themselves unconsciously behaving in hugely unethical ways against their co-workers, managers, customers or even society at large. How can culture change us at such an unconscious level?

Mats Alvesson (2002) described eight possible metaphors for studying organisational culture. He claims that culture can be viewed as: an exchange regulator; a compass; social glue; an effect regulator; disorder; blinder, or 'world closure'. Alvesson discusses the ways in which culture can produce a form of 'ethical closure'. Organisations are seen to be instruments of legal rationality, and being employed by one designates a particular set of tasks and duties that are appropriate to one's position and contract. Ethics are the concern of the individual's private life, and being professional involves leaving one's personal affairs, thoughts and concerns outside the workplace or one's dealings with customers.

Just as with the ethnographic case studies mentioned earlier in this chapter, organisational members *internalise* how they see culture being performed around them. How this process of internalisation actually works has been subject to significant debate but is widely acknowledged to have been reignited by the 1978 English language publication of Lev Vygotsky's *Mind in Society* (Zittoun & Gillespie, 2015). Vygotsky theorised that children observed that complex tasks required higher mental functions that were outside their skill set. Children first observed these at a *social* level and then made sense of it on their own terms. In order to develop practical knowledge that would help the children master these practices, the child internalises the social (or cultural) knowledge required. Passive learning about how to obtain or do things in our immediate situation, then, is critical to how culture influences our thought processes. When I first started studying in university, it seemed that everybody smoked cigarettes. The student restaurant was always filled with a thin haze of smoke and only a few tables were reserved for non-smokers. This is obviously different now, but think about what would happen if somebody sitting beside you in a café or restaurant suddenly lit up a cigarette. The fact that this scenario may be unimaginable to you demonstrates that the prohibition around smoking in shared indoor spaces in Ireland has become a *descriptive norm*: a shared cultural understanding of how things are. Shteynberg (2015) has written that descriptive norms are widely perceived to develop from the belief that an individual learns that certain activities are acceptable or moral because they have observed there to be widespread attitudinal agreement that they are ethical or normal.

Just as with mimetic desire and the civilising process, it appears that we are programmed to learn a particular way to *be* from a very young age. As adults, we move into new cultural settings all the time and are able to rationally reflect on the differences between these and the ones we have been enculturated into. How does this work when we enter new work or organisational settings as adults? One particularly useful answer is provided by a process known as *situated social learning.*

There are many different ways in which people learn things. Sometimes, we have to try to memorise important facts, but new skills and competencies also have to be acquired through practice. Learning how to do something technical, such as learning to drive a car, involves a certain amount of memorisation but is also heavily reliant on what Kolb (1984) named 'experiential learning', where we create and assimilate knowledge through experience. Kolb's model of experiential learning involves a stage of reflective observation where we observe the task to be learned (perhaps as a passenger in a car). In 1991, Jean Lavé & Etienne Wenger published *Situated Learning: Legitimate Peripheral Participation,* which explores how we learn to *be* in a particular context (such as an organisation or a workplace).

The theory of situated social learning proposes that learning often occurs as a result of certain forms of social co-participation in a particular situation. The practice of *legitimate peripheral participation* is central to situated social learning. It is legitimate because the physical presence of the learner in the context is expected or recognised by the practitioners (who are known as a *community of practice).* However, the presence of the learner is *peripheral* (at least at the outset) because the activity being undertaken is not dependent on the learner. Despite this peripheral role, the activity involves *participation* because the learner is involved in the activity, albeit in a very marginal way at first. Think of a voluntary group you may have joined. At first, you may have made your presence legitimate through an invitation from an acquaintance or an introduction. When you first joined, you may have stood back from the activities of the group in order to get a sense of what the activity involved, but gradually you became more involved and participated in the group to a greater extent. Situated social learning proposes that this is how people gradually become involved in organisational life as a cultural activity. Formal learning activities (such as attending lectures or reading prescribed texts) may impart knowledge to students, but situated social learning demonstrates how newcomers are assimilated into *communities of practice*.

There is a practical lesson from the theory of situated social learning for anyone who would like to move into management positions in the organisations that they have just joined. When we join an organisation, we often focus on making a good impression by doing the job we are hired to do to the very best of our abilities. While doing this, we often forget to take the executive sub-culture of the organisation into account. We are presented with many opportunities to observe and participate in this sub-culture, but may not be attentive to these openings when they arise. Understanding this is often key to becoming considered a potential entrant to the managerial ranks.

5: Perspectives on Ethics: Managers & Managing

Management means different things to different people. Early modern management theorists, such as F.W. Taylor (1911), perceived management as something that should be undertaken in the most scientific and quantifiable way possible, and Henri Fayol (1949) believed it to primarily involve planning, co-ordinating and controlling the work of others from a distance. Both of these theorists were products of early 20th century industrialisation and their view of management (which they felt could be universally applied to all workplaces) and the role of managers dominated management theory for some time. Since Elton Mayo's 'Hawthorne Studies' in the 1920s and 1930s, many management and organisational theorists, such as Mary Parker Follett, Peter Drucker and Douglas McGregor, advocated greater attention to the social and interactional sides of management. Henry Mintzberg's iconoclastic 1975 *Harvard Business Review* article, 'The manager's job: Folklore and fact', was a reality-check on the principles of classical management theory, which asserted that managers are primarily involved in organising, planning, co-ordinating and controlling. Mintzberg's close research on a small group of managers determined that managers actually spent most of their working day in interpersonal communication with colleagues and employees, collecting, appraising and disseminating information and making decisions.

Newly-appointed or promoted managers are often shocked to find a strong degree of resistance to their role as decision-maker. In one of the most illustrative articles on the experience of taking on the role of manager, the colourfully-titled 'Becoming manager, or the werewolf looks anxiously in the mirror, checking for unusual facial hair' (2004), Martin Parker writes of his experience of being bombarded with decisions that had been handed to him to make, and with questions about the decisions he has made. He likens the experience to being 'both the waste bin and King Solomon' (2004: 48). It is easy to see how managers in such positions find their ethics compromised in a constant onslaught of demands and interruptions.

It would be untrue to say that management is entirely scientific and rational, or completely social. I propose that management be defined as *the practical art, craft and science of getting things done with, through and for other people.* In his 1975 article, Mintzberg states that the manager plays the central role in making decisions for his/her unit, so we begin our discussion of the ethical implications of management with the ethics of managerial decision-making. We begin by examining (and critiquing) perhaps the most dominant model of ethical decision-making, before discussing alternative cultural and psychodynamic alternatives.

Managers & Ethical Decision-making

Decision-making is often not the straightforward practice suggested by classical approaches to management. Desai & Kouchaki (2017) pointed out that there is longstanding disagreement in moral psychology as to whether moral judgement is done *deliberately* (or consciously) or *automatically* (or unconsciously). In this section, we will discuss (and challenge) the main theories of the two most recognised scholars who view moral thought and behaviour as something that is deliberate. These approaches assume that decision-making is *rational*, conscious and, in organisations, oriented to providing economic results to the organisation. In many cases, however, decision-making is a political process within organisations that is socially-oriented and concerned with the distribution of power amongst different managerial actors. As such, it is often highly irrational. Rational managerial decision-making approaches are probably more useful to the practice of managing and operating complex machine systems than human beings. Rational models for making decisions assume that decision-makers make logical, rational decisions that will be in the organisation's best economic interests. They also assume that all decision-makers act to achieve known agreed goals, and problems are precisely formulated and defined. Decision-makers in such situations strive for conditions of certainty, which means that all alternatives and potential outcomes are calculated in advance of decisions being made. This is an idealised view of decision-making, because it imagines that outcomes are often programmable and that the conditions in which decisions are made are *stable*. Such stability is often little more than a fantasy and organisational life is often conducted according to cultural and political processes. With culture and politics crowding the decision space available to managers, how can they make decisions that are as ethical as possible?

Moral psychologists often propose that we develop our moral standards in a developmental fashion. In the first case, we inherit them from our immediate family. Typically (but not always), children learn what is right and wrong through fear of punishment, which Lawrence Kohlberg refers to as the *pre-conventional* stage (Reed, 1997). By the time we reach adolescence, we have internalised a basic understanding of what is right and wrong in order to meet the expectations of our friends, family and teachers, etc. (the *conventional* stage of moral development). A mature, critical re-investigation of these moral standards is often part of our transition to full adulthood (the *post-conventional* stage).

James Rest was a student of Kohlberg and, like him, was fascinated with finding answers to questions about why people developed morally in different ways. His research developed models and approaches to help people understand various elements of their moral and ethical identity. Towards the end of his career, he worked on exploring ethical development in professional fields. One of the processes he proposed was a four-step approach to making ethical decisions, which has often been discussed in relation to management and organisational scenarios (1986).

The first of these steps is the development of *moral awareness* or how much an individual is capable of understanding that a situation involves ethics or morality. In the aftermath of a failure of the capitalist system, management educators often turn to question the business schools and universities, which are somehow viewed as being complicit in the development of an unethical mindset. Sumantra Ghoshal (2005) and Henry Mintzberg (2004) proposed that an increasingly *economised focus* within business curricula resulted in the production of graduates who are socially unaware and ethically unconcerned. More recently Bergman, Westerman & Daly (2010) found that levels of narcissism amongst US college students have increased in the last 25 years or so, and this rise has been particularly pronounced in business students. Mainstream management academics have suggested that the type of education provided in business schools during the years of the global economic upturn may have contributed to this situation. By stressing that the role of business is to create profits for shareholders or managers, rather than developing value for organisations and their employees, markets or society in general, many business schools have been accused of downplaying the moral dimension of business and management. Managers are human beings and, like everyone else working in a commercial context, suffer the psychological impact of having to compromise their beliefs and values. As Leon Festinger (1957) demonstrated, when individuals fail to resolve internal conflicts, cognitive dissonance leads to stress and discomfort. Convincing individuals that organisational, and indeed social, life can be reduced to abstract economic principles may attempt to free individuals of the problems associated with having a conscience, but in truth they rarely work. Once an issue has been identified as having the potential to impact on other parties, it has become a moral concern and must be treated as such.

Rest's next step is concerned with the individual making a *moral judgement* about the ethical issue under consideration. The research literature on ethical or moral judgements has been found to be highly fragmented (Culiberg & Mihelič, 2016) so here we look at the psychological factors that contribute to an individual's moral awareness. Individuals who have a strong *internal locus of control* tend to demonstrate greater consideration of the consequences of their decision on others. People with an *external local of control*, on the other hand, not only demonstrate less consideration of the consequences of their decision on others, they also are more likely to comply with unethical actions requested from people with legitimate authority, and less likely to believe that they have a choice in relation to actions requested from those people. People who work in bureaucratic systems might be more at risk of engaging unethical behaviour as such systems can compromise an individual's sense of agency by suppressing their moral autonomy, with the result that their individual morality becomes subjugated to organisational rules. This can lead to the production of an instrumental form of morality, where the organisational member's attention is focused on the attainment of organisational goals at all costs. Eventually, employees in this position may end up engaging in removing all social elements from how they deal with subordinates, colleagues, stakeholders and customers through 'distancing' or denying a moral status to their actions. Distancing occurs when too much focus on rules ends up separating employees from the consequences of their actions. Moral status is denied when individuals are 'rendered' or understood as derivatives of organisational inputs or outputs (employees can be rendered as human resources, customers as markets, etc.).

The manager is a key ethical player in making sure that this doesn't happen. Mintzberg's classic (1975) article on the manager's job said that managers do not do particular things so much as they inhabit a set of *roles*. Two notorious sets of social psychology experiments highlight the ethical influence that being in a managerial role can have on the person being managed, and indeed the person who holds the role. The first of these was Stanley Milgram's studies of obedience, which were published as *Obedience to Authority* in 1974. Milgram was Jewish and by his early teens had developed a fascination with finding the answer to the question of why so many people were complicit with the Holocaust. Milgram solicited paid volunteers to participate in an experiment which he (misleadingly) informed them was about the impact of punishment or learning. Lots were drawn and one participant was named the 'learner' and the other the 'teacher'. The 'learner' was actually part of a deception and did not participate in the experiment. The teacher asked the learner (who the teacher believed was connected to a series of electrodes behind a dividing wall) a series of questions. As the learner gave the wrong answers, the teacher administered an electric shock from a generator. As more questions were answered wrongly, a lab-coated research assistant told the teacher to administer higher levels of shocks until the learner began to emit screams, request to be let out of the experiment, and eventually fell silent. If the teacher raised their concerns with the research assistant, they were simply told to continue. Two-thirds (65%) of the participants continued to deliver shocks on the instruction of the research assistant, even though the learner had fallen silent. The managerial implication of this is that most people comply when instructed to do something by a person in a position of authority, even though it will hurt another person.

The second example pertains to what can potentially happen when somebody is placed into an authority-related role. In 1971, Stanford University psychology professor Philip Zimbardo randomly assigned male students to the roles of prisoners or guards who would respectively be housed in, and guard, a specially constructed on-campus 'prison'. Prisoners and guards were given uniforms and Zimbardo instructed the guards to create a sense of powerlessness in the prisoners (and unwittingly created the opposite in the guards). The prisoners were 'arrested', given uniforms and assigned a number. Within the space of one week, the prisoners began to exhibit signs that they were adapting to their own debasement, while the guards rapidly demonstrated heightened levels of sadism towards the prisoners. It took the intervention of a graduate student to end the experiment mid-way through its two-week timeframe. When placed into an immersive role, individuals appear to fit their personality to it, rather than the other way around.

The ethics of both these experiments are often critiqued as both involved deception of research participants and damage to participants. From an ethical perspective, they tell us much about the moral power of the manager's role and the ability of those who hold it to change those they manage, or for it to change them. Zimbardo has more recently theorised a process that he has named 'the Lucifer Effect'

(2007), which outlines how good people can unwittingly find themselves committing evil acts.

The third step of Rest's model is the moral decision-making process when the individual or manager making the decision considers how their *ethical intentions* will be translated into action and establishes an intent to act in a particular way. At this stage, the individual decides whether and how they will act on the ethical judgement that they arrived at during the previous phase of the process. To do this, they must decide to prioritise the ethical or moral dimensions of the decision above all other elements in their reasoning process. It is important that this not be treated as a 'throwaway' decision, as it is likely to be the source of much anxiety. Anxiety is a concept that appears in much psychoanalytic theory and is often a key factor in contributing the evolution of organisational processes and practices. Ironically, these practices and processes, which are supposed to defend employees and managers from anxiety, can be just as damaging to them as the anxiety they are trying to avoid. Anxiety is a very normal and natural emotion to experience and, in many ways, it can drive us to address underlying fears and fix personal and social problems. Students who have prepared for an examination and feel very anxious before taking it, for example, are probably in a better state of preparedness than those who feel no anxiety at all. Individuals who experience anxiety to the extent that it is debilitating or damaging to their mental health should, of course, seek immediate medical assistance.

In social and organisational settings, anxiety manifests in very different ways and it is important to separate the psychoanalytic understanding of anxiety from the normal fear or discomfort that individuals might experience from time to time. All sources of anxiety are both painful and part of our conscious world: when we feel anxious, we *know* that we are anxious. Because anxiety is so unpleasant to experience, we are strongly motivated to stop the painful anguish we experience. Anxiety alerts the ego to deal with external, conscious or unconscious sources of danger. If these sources of danger are not addressed, anxieties can accumulate and cause the individual to breakdown. Freud differentiated between three main interrelated forms of anxiety: *reality* (or *objective*) anxiety; *neurotic* anxiety and *moral* anxiety (Hall, 1954).

Reality anxiety stems from our experiences of encountering threats in the real world. These often occur in early childhood, when our negative experiences might have been more traumatic due to our inability to help ourselves at the time. As a result of experiencing helplessness, many people retain a sense of fear about particular objects that caused an anxiety-creating experience when they were very young (such as a fear of dogs, for example). Freud wrote that the trauma involved in the experience of being born 'has become the prototype of the effects of a mortal danger' (1974: 444). In other words, when we become highly anxious, we re-live the feelings of complete helplessness that we felt when we underwent the trauma of birth.

Neurotic anxiety may stem from actual experiences or threats that people may have encountered, but have become instilled in the *id*. We are fearful, in other words, of what our unconscious instincts might cause us to do. This manifests in different ways. *Free-floating* anxiety, for example, is a general sense of dread that bad things will happen to us. A Freudian analyst might say that this is the result of an individual being wary of what their unconscious mind might cause them to do. In the organisational case study by Casey (1999) mentioned in the previous chapter, the implementation of a team-based culture dispersed anxiety throughout groups in a free-floating way rather than having it centred in one employee-manager relationship. *Phobias* are fears of certain objects or things, and Freudian theory suggests that they develop because we actually desire these (often forbidden) objects at an unconscious level. As with all objects of neurotic anxiety, our desire to repress them through fleeing or neutralising them can often backfire and develop into neuroses that become part of our personalities, which if not addressed can hold us back from reaching our full potential.

Moral anxiety is the final main form of anxiety mentioned by Freud and is experienced by feelings of guilt or shame brought on us by our own superego. The stronger a person's superego (which Freud wrote is usually influenced by our parent figures or other morally important individuals or institutions in our upbringing), the more likely they are to experience

intense feelings of guilt about things that others may not experience. Hall
(1954) has written of the irony of 'virtuous' people experiencing more
shame than the 'unvirtuous' and claims that some people commit crimes
out of a sense of guilt that has led to them wanting to be caught and
punished in order to restore their inner equilibrium.

With so many different possible sources of guilt and anxiety
influencing our inner lives, it is clear to see that the act of clearly
establishing our ethical intentions is not straightforward. Anxiety is so
unpleasant that it usually activates defence mechanisms such as
repression, denial, rationalisation, projection and displacement, etc.
(Gabriel & Carr, 2002). This is mirrored in work organisations, which
can be viewed from a psychological perspective as being designed to
manage anxiety in particular ways. Senior managers appoint a unit
manager who is responsible for the outputs and resources used by her
department. The anxiety attached to running that department is
displaced to a manager who must then, in turn, pass this anxiety to
various supervisors and staff members. If any part of the system fails to
deliver, the organisational 'superego' will demand punishment. Fears of
external or internal threats are formulated through rules and
procedures; from a psychoanalytic perspective, these might be viewed
as neurotic constraints that seek to contain anxiety but actually stifle
spontaneity and innovation. Organisational defences against anxiety
are self-defeating, because they either only address the source of the
anxiety in a superficial and unsustainable way (Hyde & Thomas, 2002)
or result in the issue being over-managed in a manner that actually gets
in the way of tasks being completed.

Anxiety, then, is clearly a managerial concern. In attempting to
defend themselves, their staff and their organisations from anxiety,
managers can inadvertently increase it or introduce pathological
processes that cause valuable staff to disengage from the organisation
or work unit. Many studies of organisational anxiety cite a landmark
study by Isabel Menzies (1960), which found that a large number of
high-performing nurses left a teaching hospital due to the rigid
structures and processes that had been put in place to keep the reality
of human suffering at a distance. The nurses left because they felt they

could not nurse due to the organisational defences against anxiety that had been put in place. Organisational psychoanalysis often speaks of the importance of 'containing' anxiety in a particular space, process or unit that allows it to be distanced from employees (James & Clark, 2002). These containers (management, the board, etc.) allow organisational members to project their anxieties in the form of blame somewhere outside themselves and their own responsibilities. When organisations change, these containers often disappear and anxiety is released into the organisation. Grint (2005), for example, discusses leaders as *containers* of their followers' anxieties. In Casey's (1999) case, the introduction of team-based working effectively reconfigured the role of the leader into the role of the professional; suddenly teams found themselves containing anxieties that were previously projected elsewhere in the organisation.

The final step of Rest's model is to *act morally* when undertaking the action that has been decided upon. The role of anxiety in management and organisational life demonstrates that this is far more complicated than rational decision-making theory suggests. In a remarkable recent article, Moxnes (2017) offers a perspective on anxiety that can be useful for managers in how they organise and motivate groups. Moxnes recognises that organisational structures can create anxiety, alienate high-performing individuals and constrain creativity, but also points out that the removal of existing structures also creates anxiety. The lesson is that employees react to structured situations in different ways, so it is important to understand these reaction types and ensure that an *appropriate* amount of structure is applied. Some groups are oriented towards 'socio-processual' behaviour, such as establishing a formal goal and following an agenda and procedures towards an established end; others prefer 'psycho-process behaviour', which is open, exploratory, creative and leaderless. Individuals with high 'socio-needs' will find working with 'psycho-groups' very stressful and *vice versa*. Understanding the unconscious needs of group members can assist managers to understand why different types of groups perform better in different circumstances.

Although the four stages of Rest's model appear to be directly interrelated, it is important to note that the processes states that each stage must be engaged with independently to execute ethical decision-making in full. O'Fallon & Butterfield (2005) and Craft (2013) reviewed the empirical research literature on ethical decision-making and found Rest's framework to have maintained a position of prominence. Jones (1991) has demonstrated how several theorists have built on Rest's four-component model of ethical theory in various ways, which has extended it beyond personal awareness of the moral nature of a situation to include situational, environmental, social, organisational, legal and other factors. Jones introduced a new concept, *moral intensity,* which he postulated could be used to analyse every ethical issue. Jones was concerned with why people responded differently to moral issues, and believed that these responses were based on the characteristics of the issue that was being grappled with. Jones proposed that *moral intensity* was made up of six components that he listed as: magnitude of consequences; social consequences; probability of effect; temporal immediacy; proximity; and concentration of effect (1991).

How useful are these models are in practice? This chapter began by discussing the thoughts of theorists on the position of managers as involving almost constant communication from a variety of stakeholders with very little time for reflection. When faced with constant demands on their time and mental energy, do managers really have time to sit down and use models to determine just how they feel in relation to ethical or moral conundrums that impact on them? Barraquier (2011) found most research on ethical decision-making to be dominated by rationalist perspectives that ultimately fail to provide a comprehensive picture of how managers make decisions. Throughout the discussion of Rest's model in this chapter, examples of theories and approaches that might support or critique this model have been provided. Some alternative approaches to ethical decision-making for managers have stressed that individuals can achieve cognitive consistency when faced with moral dilemmas by first clarifying for themselves what they are 'about' in terms of their values or their own personal philosophical stance. It is important for the manager to do this in order to avoid sustaining a *moral injury*.

GUILT & MORAL INJURY

When I first began teaching business ethics, I was delighted to have a chance to move into a challenging area that had genuine potential to not only change the way in which managers and businesses worked, but also to help students attain new understandings of themselves and their potential to affect progressive change in the world. However, I found many of the existing textbooks to be of limited value because they were either too *negative*, *prescriptive* or *affirmative* about the field of business ethics. Negative approaches to business ethics either adopted a condemnatory stance towards businesses or managers whom, the authors deemed, had acted in an unethical way. Others took a more critical stance that viewed the entire practice of capitalistic enterprise to be essentially unsound and argued that it should be abandoned in favour of another system. Approaches that were too *prescriptive* merely described ways in which managers or organisations could 'be' ethical (and many of these appeared impractical). *Affirmative* approaches celebrated the efforts of organisations to be more sustainable, ethical or socially responsible. Whereas all of these are important aspects of studying the relationship between business, ethics and society, I became concerned they would not allow an understanding of the topic as it relates to the everyday experience of managers, managing and being managed. In short, I found that most of these approaches applauded or vilified managers as *conscious* creators of moral or immoral behaviour and circumstances. Ernest Becker's work (mentioned in **Chapter 1**) points out that most people do not set out to be immoral, and many people who create acts of evil simply believe that they are acting morally. Given the huge influence that unconscious forces have on our thoughts and actions, we need to consider why there are many people who have unconsciously committed acts of evil or immorality in a way that has later horrified them when they because consciously aware of what they have done.

In organisational life, this often arises from the strong influence that organisational culture can have on our own agency, as described in the previous chapter. Sometimes this results from making poor decisions that have caused losses, which in turn leads to a downward spiral of increasingly immoral actions in order to try to dig oneself out of the problems created (which is often the case of 'rogue traders' trying to escape losses they have incurred). In other cases, managers find themselves personally compromised by making decisions in the interest of their organisations that have hurt stakeholders, employees, or even their own families. These effects are often only recognised when we momentarily catch a glimpse of ourselves through the eyes of other people and don't like what we see. We ask ourselves how we came to do things that we find morally repulsive, and how we have become such an immoral person. In some cases, such moments of clarity are the path to self-reappraisal and reality-checking that help us to 'morally' get back on track.

An example of this was Ray C. Anderson, who founded one of the largest carpet manufacturers in the world, Interface Inc. According to Anderson's autobiography, *Mid-Course Correction* (1999), Interface organised a task force to respond to customer concerns about the natural environment, and Anderson was invited to make a keynote address to it. In preparation, he read Paul Hawken's *The Ecology of Commerce (1993)* and was deeply distressed by the account of businesses culpability in the destruction of natural world. Anderson describes the impact of this work on him in almost violent terms; he talks of being 'hit between the eyes' and feeling 'a spear in his chest'. As a result, he set about making Interface not just a sustainable company, but also a *restorative* company that contributed to the renewal of the natural environment.

Becoming conscious of the unethical or unsustainable behaviours we were previously unconscious of can result in personal and organisational redemption in many cases. Cases where this is not possible, where irreparable damage has been done and irreversible pain inflicted, perhaps emphasise the importance of developing an awareness of the unconscious forces that can work in our lives. Several studies of genocide have demonstrated that a myriad number of historical, social, political and psychological forces shape the mindset of killers in genocide (Browning, 2001). Despite the reasons for people becoming mindlessly violent, the individuals who commit atrocities have to live with their actions afterwards when they 'return to their senses'. Many of the Hutu killers who participated in the Rwandan genocide over a three-month period in 1994 and brutally killed their innocent Tutsi neighbours have recounted immense remorse over their actions. They discuss becoming animalistic, losing their self-identity, not recognising themselves or their actions and consequently suffering immense guilt when they became conscious of what they had done (Hatzfeld, 2005; Migiro, 2014).

This idea of our unconscious minds containing forces that can unexpectedly manifest and destabilise our lives has long been explored in art. Psychotherapy and psychoanalysis aim to help individuals find the unseen forces in an individual's subconscious to help them recover from their mental distress and to prevent them for abruptly disrupting an individual's everyday life and harming those who they live or work with. This is a key theme in one of Freud's most controversial theories: the notorious 'Oedipus complex'. In psychoanalytic theory, a complex is a jumble of emotions, beliefs and drives that exist around a thought or group of thoughts. For example, an individual or a team might constantly sabotage their own success as a result of a complex that they have about achievement. As such complexes are pathological, it is important to discover the forces and experiences that might have influenced their development in order to overcome them. Freud was fascinated with the myth of Oedipus, particularly as it was dramatised by the Greek tragedian, Sophocles.

When Oedipus was born, his parents, King Laius and Queen Jocasta, were informed by an oracle that he would grow up to kill his father and marry his mother. Horrified, the queen ordered that he be abandoned on a mountain, but he was found and adopted by another king and queen. When he was older, Oedipus leaned about the prophecy about himself and left the kingdom to avoid fulfilling it. He argued with a wealthy man and his retinue on the road, and killed the man and most of his entourage. The wealthy man, unknown to him, was his real father, King Laius. Oedipus later freed the city state of Thebes from a ravaging monster (the Sphinx) by solving a riddle. As a reward, Oedipus was offered the hand of the recently-widowed Queen Jocasta in marriage. He went on to have children with Jocasta and ruled Thebes until it was struck by a famine and disease. A messenger arrived from Corinth to inform Oedipus that his father had died. Oedipus' happiness at the failure of the prophecy soon ends when the messenger tells Oedipus that he was actually a shepherd who was responsible for abandoning him as a baby, but instead had passed him to the childless royal family of Corinth. Oedipus persists in questioning the messenger and learns the truth: he has, in fact, unknowingly killed his own father and committed incest with his mother. Devastated, Oedipus blinds himself and Queen Jocasta takes her own life.

In our world, Sophocles' play *Oedipus Rex* would not be considered a tragedy; it would be viewed as an extreme horror story. Contemporary horror films are perhaps one of the best manifestations of the process by which individuals are tormented by suddenly forces that have suddenly been freed from a realm that we didn't previously know existed. Horror movies frighten us because unseen forces suddenly emerge from unexpected places to attack our daily lives. Once the unseen force has been revealed and explained, its power to scare viewers is greatly reduced (which explains why horror and thriller sequels often do not retain their ability to scare audiences).

Freud used Sophocles' telling of the Oedipus myth in two ways. First, he saw it as having deep significance for the psychosexual development of children. At a very young age, little boys, he theorised, were attracted to their mothers and hated their fathers, wanting to usurp them and take their place as their mother's partner. As the boy grows up, he represses these feelings and develops a sense of guilt about them (facilitating the development of the superego). Freud's Oedipus complex theory served to underpin his theories about sexual development in children and related ideas about latency, castration anxiety in males, penis envy in females and relationship with parents. These ideas were, and remain, deeply controversial and contested to this day. However, there is another element to his interest in the Oedipus story that isn't discussed as much. In the play, he found an analogy for the way in which we repress traumatic experiences to the extent that we don't remember them anymore. Like Oedipus, we eventually become blind to them. Just because we are no longer aware of them, however, does not mean that they cease to exist. In fact, because we have repressed them in our unconscious, they have the ability to arise in forms that we do not anticipate. Freud suggested that this was one of the main reasons why the Oedipus story had been told and re-enacted many times since the ancient Greeks poets and dramatists first accounted for it. We can see this in the plotlines of some contemporary horror films and thriller novels, where the hero of the film actually learns that they are really the villain of the story.

One particularly interesting manifestation of this as it relates to management, leadership and organisational life is the concept of the *moral injury* (or 'moral wound'). The American psychiatrist Jonathan Shay, who is most closely associated with this idea, worked with US veterans and their psychological problems dealing with guilt and social reintegration following their return from active service. Shay has challenged the idea that all ex-soldiers' difficulties arise from trying to process the horrors they have witnessed or participated in during wartime. Rather than experiencing what has become commonly known as post-traumatic stress disorder (PTSD), Shay proposed the idea that ex-servicemen and servicewomen experience a 'moral injury' when they are forced to violate their own moral beliefs during times of extreme tension, either through their own actions (Litz *et al*, 2009) or through the orders of somebody in command (Shay, 1994). The impact of these moral violations often manifest for years afterwards (Shay, 2002), making the life of the veterans deeply troubled for themselves and for those around them. Moral injuries result in deterioration of an individual's moral character, even though they felt that they may have needed to commit them to survive at a particular time. Thomas E. Allen (2014) has suggested that many outside therapeutic practice have used the term 'moral wound', as opposed to 'moral injury', as wounding can leave scars that can last for a long time. What is wounded, according to

Allen, is the *ego-ideal* (mentioned in **Chapter 4**): the idealised self that we have constructed for ourselves or that has been constructed for us, and which we strive to live up to. Allen (2014) discusses his interviews with military recruits who aspire to join the Army to serve society, travel and/or acquire a profession or education. Many do not think about the fundamental societal, ethical or religious prohibition against taking another human life, and are morally wounded when faced with actually doing so.

The key learning from this, as can be seen in Ray Anderson's story, is that not being aware of our own deeply held ethical frameworks can lead us to unintentionally transgress them. Not knowing what these frameworks, values and beliefs were does not save us from devastating guilt and pain after the violation has been committed (although many clinical psychologists, psychiatrists and psychoanalysts continue to make great strides in healing moral injuries and repairing moral wounds). The world of work and organisations is full of opportunities to succeed and progress, but sometimes these opportunities come at the cost of violating one's personal values and ethical frameworks. Managers, whose position in organisations lie at a point between the needs of directors and shareholders and the staff they manage, are often most at risk of experiencing moral wounds, but are also ideally placed to prevent moral injuries to their staff, their organisations and themselves. It perhaps goes without saying that, to avoid guilt and moral injury, or to recover from unknowingly acquiring a moral wound, managers and employees should develop a deep awareness of their own value system or moral foundation.

VALUES, MORAL FOUNDATIONS & MANAGERS

In the section in this chapter titled 'Managers & Ethical Decision-making', it was mentioned that there is a debate in the field of moral psychology as to whether our moral choices and actions are deliberate (conscious) or automatic (or unconscious) (Desai & Kouchaki, 2017). In that section, we looked at the deliberate school of thought, and discussed it in relation to psychoanalysis. In this section, we look at some approaches that try to understand the processes by which individuals reach moral judgements in a way which is immediate, automatic and unconscious.

Moral psychology asserts that, as individuals, we have moral identities that are concerned with the extent to which an individual's self-concept and behaviour include characteristically moral traits. As we are motivated to maintain psychological consistency, when we commit ethical violations we are motivated to disengage from moral self-sanctions. We do this through processes of cognitive reconstruals (where we find some form of moral justification for our behaviour or through sanitising the language that we might have used). Individuals also attempt to balance their moral identity with ethical violations by minimising their personal causal agency (or sense of personal responsibility) by placing blame on other parties or diffusing responsibility to other areas. This desire to adhere to moral principles or values is key to an individual's sense of personal integrity. An especially dangerous means of balancing moral identity with violations is the practice of distorting or disregarding harmful consequences arising from an action, which can involve perpetrators of ethical mis-deeds blaming or de-valuing their victims.

Milton Rokeach defined values as 'enduring belief[s] that a specific mode of conduct is personally or socially preferable to an opposite or converse mode of conduct or end-state or existence' (1973: 5). Rokeach identified two different groupings of values, which can then be sub-divided into two further types.

The first of these is desirable modes of conduct (or *instrumental* values). There are two types of instrumental value:

o **Moral values:** Concerned with behaviours that individuals consider right or wrong; and

o **Competence values:** Concerned with values that assist an individual to self-actualise.

The second group of values that Rokeach identified was desirable end states of existence (or *terminal* values). As with instrumental values, terminal values can be further divided into:

o **Personal values:** Things that an individual wants for themselves; and

o **Social values:** Things an individual wants for other people.

Rokeach identified 18 terminal values. It is important to note that Rokeach pointed out that there were no underlying relationships between one type of instrumental value and another end value. In other words, just because you have ranked a certain instrumental value as of most importance to yourself, it does not necessarily follow that you will have a 'corresponding' terminal value.

Many theorists who view ethics as being more socially constructed than deliberate do so by challenging the theories of Lawrence Kohlberg, mentioned above, and this is certainly the case with the two moral psychologists, Carol Gilligan and Jonathan Haidt. Gilligan's incredible work will be discussed in the next chapter in relation to stakeholder theory. Jonathan Haidt's work has become very influential in recent years, not only because of the challenges it offers to more deterministic models of ethical decision-making but because of its applicability to the changing political landscape. In *The Righteous Mind* (2012), Haidt challenges the developmental view of morality as it proposes that we determine what is right or wrong on an individual basis. Rather than seeing ethical decision-making as rational, Haidt proposes that it is mainly emotional. We react to ethical violations immediately and automatically on the basis of how feel about them. The process of moral reasoning, according to Haidt, is only really engaged with on a social level to try to bring other people around to our point of view.

Rather than proposing that these intuitive reactions are innate to everyone, Haidt demonstrates that different cultures have distinct moral 'triggers' that value certain things above others and cause dissonance when they have been violated. These are based on moral foundations that stem from the adaptive challenges faced by our ancestors. Although the reasons for these reactions might have changed over the years, they serve to inform us about what is virtue and vice depending on the moral foundation that influence us. We have a tendency to ignore or discredit information that runs counter to the moral foundations that we adhere to.

Haidt's *moral foundations theory* (2012) asserts that there are six main moral foundations. The *care/harm* foundation emerged from a social need to protect the vulnerable young of a society. As babies learn to observe others from a very young stage of their development, we learn to value caring and being cared for from an early part of our life. The *fairness/cheating* moral foundation stems from a cultural unit's need to have active co-operation and partnerships. This moral foundation values virtues such as fairness and trust and makes us suspicious of social loafers and individuals who benefit from systems in a way that is disproportionate to what they have contributed to them. The *loyalty/betrayal* foundation recognises the importance of remaining loyal to a group and to be suspicious of all attempts to undermine its social basis or legitimacy. The *authority/subversion* foundation sees the beneficial potential of being obedient to hierarchical structures in order to protect the group, particularly as they serve to stave off potential chaos. The *sanctity/degradation* foundation stems from a society's need to protect itself from physical or social contamination that it perceives to arise from outside the group. Finally, the *liberty/oppression* foundation emerges from concerns that the structural benefits arising from the loyalty/betrayal or authority/subversion moral foundations can be abused by individuals who become too powerful and lead to societies that are too unequal. Totalitarian societies are difficult to sustain as they are always at risk of being toppled by those they do not benefit as members. The resources required to police and oppress individuals can become so large that insurrection and rebellion become inevitable.

It is interesting to see how these different moral foundations play out in social and political life. Groups are condemned by other groups for violating the moral foundations that they value, but all do so from the perspective that they themselves are doing the 'right thing'. Ethical decisions, according to the moral foundations theory, are made automatically for unconscious cultural reasons and are only 'rationalised' when we try to communicate them to other people.

What does this mean for the individual employee then who is asked by a manager to violate their own moral foundations by committing what they believe to be an ethical violation? In our workplaces, we often find ourselves in situations where our moral responsibilities might clash with our work responsibilities and having to resolve clashes between these two may prove problematic. The simplest way to do this is not to be put in this position in the first place. If we are clear what our moral foundations are, and about what we cannot compromise, we can communicate this to managers in a way that is not perceived as aggressive or 'preachy'. Desai & Kochaki (2017) describe the process of deploying moral symbols (such as words, phrases, images or objects) that clarify one's own ethical position in a safe and non-confrontational way in order to prime managers about the moral values of their employees. Employees' clothing and worn religious symbols or the books, posters or symbols adorning their office space, their espoused membership of organised groups or the stories of moral courage they tell can not only clarify their own value system, but can even influence the behaviour and attitudes of their co-workers and managers. Desai & Kouchaki (2017) refer to the use of moral symbols by employees as acting as a 'necklace of garlic' that protects employees from behaving unethically.

In the following chapter, we will explore stakeholder theory as it relates to the field of business and management and will explore Carol Gilligan's important contribution to the concept of ethic of care.

6: Ethics as Strategy: Stakeholder Theory & Management

So far, this book has focused on the individual as an ethical actor in organisational life. From this point on, it examines how organisations as a whole engage with ethics. As in the first part of the book, we approach the organisation from the *outside*: we start with its stakeholders and move inwards to the various corporate and political bodies that steer and regulate the behaviour of the organisation. In the following chapters, we examine how businesses engage with issues such as globalisation, international development, environmental degradation, social change and consider the role of leadership in safeguarding the ethical climate and culture of business. First, however, we examine the role of stakeholders in organisational life.

Stakeholder Theory & Strategy

The discipline of strategy has long emphasised the centrality of the concept of competitive advantage. Indeed, leading textbooks, such as Johnson *et al*'s *Exploring Corporate Strategy* (2005), define strategy as the general long-term direction an organisation chooses to take in order to meet the expectations of stakeholders. Mainstream strategic theory tends to view stakeholders as groups that are mutually dependent on the organisation. Few internal stakeholders are perceived as having sufficient power to determine the strategy of an organisation, but several stakeholders in the market (such as suppliers, distributors, competitors and shareholders), the socio-political milieu (government agencies, policy-makers and regulators) and in the field of technology (key adaptors, standards agencies, etc.) are often acknowledged as being important parties whose views must be considered by organisations during planning. This acknowledgement of stakeholders in strategic and business theory has much to do with R. Edward Freeman's stakeholder approach to strategic management, which first became popular in the early 1980s. In the Foreword to *Strategic Management: A Stakeholder Perspective*, Freeman (2010) advocated such a stakeholder approach as a response to the significant changes facing North American businesses at that time.

Freeman (2010) defined stakeholders as being a person or group who could influence or impact, or be impacted by, the way a firm achieves its objectives. At the core of his stakeholder management theory is a realisation (achieved from the various contributions made by strategic [or corporate] planning theory, systems theory, corporate social responsibility, and organisational theory) that stakeholders in the organisation's environment are critical to its ability to exist and prosper. Where previous models of organisational design (such as production and managerial-based views of the firm) placed the environment outside a boundary to be managed, Freeman instead saw these environmental elements as being core to how the firm determines what it is for.

Freeman advocated that successful stakeholder management be based on the principles of *voluntarism*: an organisation must decide to develop relationships with its stakeholders *itself* (without coercion or reward). He described his approach as *enterprise strategy*: the moral or ethical level of strategy (which is usually ignored by mainstream strategy). He saw enterprise strategy to be concerned with identifying the relationship of the firm with society and asking what the firm stands for.

Strategic Management: A Stakeholder Approach was one of the first texts to establish how businesses should listen to the concerns of those who were not in a direct position to influence the ability to generate profit. It contains several models, neologisms and a range of processes to assist managers 'do' strategy with stakeholders. From these processes, Freeman proposed that organisations could select one of five generic enterprise strategies. The first of these was to choose to maximise benefits to *one stakeholder group*, or to a small set of stakeholders. Related to this were strategies that that sought to maximise benefits to *stockholders only*. This second strategy was probably the most prevalent stakeholder strategy in mainstream corporate life at that time. The third strategy aims to maximise benefits to *all stakeholders* and improve the average welfare of all parties in society. The fourth aimed to maximise benefits to *the 'worst-off' stakeholder*, which in turn would result in the position of all stakeholders being raised (in theory). The final strategy aimed to achieve consensus between the organisation and all its stakeholders with the aim of creating and maintaining social harmony. Freeman named the first strategy a *specific stakeholder strategy*, and the second a *stockholder strategy*. The third strategy was a *utilitarian strategy*, while the fourth strategy Freeman named a *Rawlsian* strategy and the final one a social *harmony strategy*.

It is worth elaborating on what is meant by a 'Rawlsian' strategy. John Rawls' *A Theory of Justice* (1971) is concerned with the *social contract* that individuals have with the State of which they are a citizen or subject. Many religions refer back to a time when there was a 'Golden Age', when people lived in harmony with each other and the earth and private property did not exist. Human beings became (or were) corrupted by wanting more than was given to them and grew jealous of each other. As a result, they became violent, possessive and greedy and began to fight with each other. Finally, realising that chaos and greed ultimately achieved nothing but pain, individuals agreed to co-operate with the divine and with each other. There are many myths about the origin of civilisation, but they all demonstrate a fundamental belief about the behaviour of human beings in social settings: without a firm commitment to the maintenance of civilisation, we revert to a dangerous state. There is a need, then, for *social contracts* where individuals agree to live in ways that are not harmful to each other and to obey laws. Doing this means that individuals will benefit from social cohesion and safety, but must give up certain freedoms.

There are, of course, problems inherent in living according to a social contract. The most obvious stems from the fear that the concerns of individuals will be subordinated to the needs of elite groups in society. Certainly, one of the main issues that many individuals had during the imposition of 'austerity' measures during the last global recession was that the needs of the many were subordinated to the needs of the very few rich. As the global economy was heavily *financialised*, didn't the fixing of this system mean that power had to be returned to those with most financial power? Rawls' *A Theory of Justice* addresses this concern by exploring how a fair system could be developed. He asks us to consider the behaviour of an imaginary group called the *original position*, which is charged with developing just principles by which society will be ruled. These people must determine these rules from behind a 'veil of ignorance'; none of them know the position of other people in the group, or what role they might end up fulfilling in society. Like a lucky-dip in a fairground, nobody knows what they, or the other person, are going to get. As a result, the rule of society and economy will be oriented towards the needs of the person or group who are most disadvantaged.

Since Freeman first proposed this approach to making stakeholders central to the development of strategy, stakeholder theory has undergone significant development, particularly in relation to how stakeholders are defined and both their (and the firm's) actions and responses. The performance of firms that engage with stakeholders is often considered and debates continue about the nature of stakeholder theory itself (Laplume *et al*, 2008). Stakeholder theory has undergone such significant reappraisal that it often looks substantially different to that first proposed by Freeman. Freeman has acknowledged that, although his original models were very much 'of the time' when his text was first written, one of the most significant contributions he made was the acknowledgement of the stakeholder as a significant player in developing advantages for firms. Businesses that do not create opportunities for connecting with those whose interests are important to their firms are at risk of being unsustainable in the future.

Critics of Rawlsian advocacy of maximising returns to the least well-off stakeholder have pointed out that such positions are aspirational, rather than realistic. It is worth bearing in mind that Rawls' discussion is a theoretical one that aims to assist parties to ascertain what is fair and just for all. As people interested in business and management, however, we are left with the problems of:

o Identifying who our stakeholders are;

o Answering what influence they should be allowed to have; and

o Determining how we can facilitate their participation in organisational life.

DEVELOPMENTS IN STAKEHOLDER THEORY

In 2008, André Laplume, Karan Sonpar and Reginald Litz published the first detailed overview of stakeholder theory, and noted that it had grown to a position of prominence within ethical management theory since the mid-1990s. A more recent review (Cullen, 2017) found that, alongside 'sustainability', the field of stakeholder theory had grown to be one of the largest business and society frameworks. Laplume *et al* identified five key themes where stakeholder theory had undergone the most substantial level of development: the definition and salience of stakeholders; stakeholder actions and responses; organisational actions and responses; firm performance; and debates and disagreements about stakeholder theory.

Laplume *et al* (2008) found that debates about theory accounted for most of the published output on stakeholder theory. Perhaps this is not surprising; Freeman's own undergraduate degree was in philosophy and mathematics and his doctorate was in philosophy, and many of the critiques of stakeholder theory are made on philosophical grounds and are concerned with the ethical foundations of stakeholder theory.

Laplume *et al* (2008) report that most studies find instrumental stakeholder theory has a positive relationship with firm financial performance. Indeed, this is one of the major concerns of what has become known as instrumental stakeholder theory (Egels-Zanden &

Sandberg, 2010) that was identified by Donaldson and Preston (1995). Donaldson & Preston distinguished three main aspects of research on stakeholder theory. The first of these is the *descriptive* aspect, which illustrates how organisations can be best understood from the perspective of their relationships with stakeholders. The second is the *normative* aspect, which makes claims for how stakeholders *should* be incorporated into management decisions and organisational life. The final is the *instrumental* aspect, which discusses *how* to 'do' stakeholder management.

Although theoretical debates on stakeholder management theory have received more coverage in the research literature, the area of stakeholder identification and salience remains central (Berman & Johnson-Cramer, 2016). This area is specifically concerned with answering the question of 'Which stakeholders do, and should, managers pay attention to?'. 'Toward a theory of stakeholder identification and salience: Defining the principle of who and what really counts', a 1997 paper by Ronald Mitchell, Bradley Agle and Donna Wood, is a seminal piece of work on the subject (Schwartz, 2006) whose findings have secured solid empirical support (Laplume *et al*, 2008).

Mitchell *et al* (1997) reviewed studies on stakeholders and proposed that there are different classes of stakeholders based on their possession of one, two or all of three key attributes. The first of these attributes is the stakeholders' *power* to exert an influence on the organisation. Power, in itself, is a difficult concept to define but, in the context of stakeholder theory, it refers to the ability of one group or party (stakeholders, for example) to get another group or party (a firm, for example) to do something that it would otherwise not do, or does not want to do. Mitchell *et al* refer to Etzioni's (1964) typology of three types of power: *coercive power* was based on the use of physical force, such as violence and restraint; utilitarian power applied material means, such as financial rewards to elicit desired responses; and *normative-based power* relied on symbolic rewards, such as social esteem or acceptance for the achievement of aims.

The second key attribute identified by Mitchell *et al* (1997) is the *legitimacy* of the stakeholder's relationship with the organisation. When legitimacy is combined with *power*, the result is *authority*, but it is important that we are clear about legitimacy as a standalone concept in stakeholder theory. When a stakeholder or its claim is recognised as legitimate, it means that it is perceived as desirable or appropriate to society's broader values and norms. The legitimacy of a stakeholder's claims, then, is much broader than the stakeholder or the organisation. Legitimacy is not conferred on it by the organisation or the stakeholder; it is constructed by society.

The third key attribute is the *urgency* of the stakeholders' claim on the organisation. Mitchell *et al* introduced the element of time to stakeholder considerations to capture the temporal element of organisational life. Stakeholders are aware that they can possess assets that have an in-built 'sell-by' date, which impacts on their utility to organisations. If an issue is urgent, any delay by managers in attending to the stakeholders' claim on the organisation will be deemed unacceptable by the stakeholder.

When these attributes are considered together, they produce differing degrees of *salience* or the extent to which managers give priority to some stakeholder concerns over others. If stakeholders possess only one of the key attributes, they are known as *latent* stakeholders and have a low level of salience. Stakeholders who only have a high level of *power* are known as *dormant* stakeholders because they could potentially impose their will on an organisation if they had a legitimate relationship with the firm or an urgent claim on it. Stakeholders who solely have a high level of *legitimacy* are known as *discretionary stakeholders* because they can be assisted by the organisation if it decides to do so. They have no power or urgent claims on the organisation's time or resources, so the organisation can choose to help them in a socially responsible or a philanthropic way if it chooses to do so. When the only relevant attribute of the stakeholder-manager relationship is *urgency*, the stakeholder is a *demanding* stakeholder. Although *demanding* stakeholders can be an irritant or embarrassment to managers in organisations, they do not automatically provide a threat to an organisation in achieving its aims.

If stakeholders possess two of the key attributes, they have a moderate level of salience. Because they expect something from the organisation, they are known as *expectant* stakeholders. Where these stakeholders possess both *power* and *legitimacy*, they are part of the dominant coalition (such as the board of directors) that are highly influential in the firm, and receive serious attention from managers. Stakeholders who possess *legitimacy* and *urgency* are classified as *dependent* stakeholders because they depend on the power held by other stakeholders to impose their will on the organisation. Forming coalitions with powerful *dormant* stakeholders has the potential to change these dormant stakeholders into *definitive* stakeholders (see below). Finally, where an expectant stakeholder has power and possesses urgency, but does not have legitimacy, they become *dangerous* stakeholders who can use strong, coercive tactics in an attempt to impose their will on the organisation. The dangerous stakeholder opens up some interesting questions for organisations. Should an organisation accommodate a stakeholder who has been so identified on the basis of the potential threat they provide, or are there ways in which it can identify and interact with such stakeholders in order to change their classification?

When stakeholders possess all three attributes, they are known as *definitive* stakeholders, and as such there is no question about their importance to the organisation. Because they are members of the dominant coalition that influences organisational life with an urgent concern, they are imbued with a level of stakeholder salience that means their concerns receive most of the organisational managers' attention. It also means that, if other stakeholders acquire the other key attributes, they can increase their salience to managers. On the other hand, it also demonstrates that the key attributes are themselves dynamic, and that external forces can change the level of influence that it is possible to levy on an organisation. Power can wane, urgencies are, by their nature, temporary and societal norms change, which means that what was once deemed legitimate in terms of behaviours, beliefs and activities is not set in stone. For example, one difficulty that the various environmental movements around the world faced for some time was the lack of power, legitimacy and urgency for their claims. In recent years, there has been a huge turning away from the idea that climate change is a myth. Powerful individuals in business, political, social and religious life have stressed that the damage being done to the natural world is the biggest threat to human life on this planet. Scientific findings have bolstered a broader social consensus that this damage must stop, as we have a decreasing amount of time available to us to stop polluting the natural environment the way we have been doing lest human existence is forced to undergo significant changes.

It was mentioned above that some stakeholders are classified as *discretionary* because they can be assisted at the organisation's discretion. Having no power or urgency claims on the firm, the organisation will accrue few direct benefits from assisting such stakeholders. Any such assistance is usually classified as *corporate social responsibility*.

Mitchell *et al's* model offers managers a tool for determining which shareholders should get the most attention. This may appear to be something of a brutal tool in determining why some stakeholders get attention and others do not, but it is worthwhile remembering that since many definitions of a stakeholder can be very broad and inclusive, it has the potential to enable managers to include stakeholders in their decision-making, rather than excluding them as an unmanageable distraction. Indeed, many normative stakeholder theories stem from the belief that *all* the interests of *all* stakeholders are of intrinsic value (Donaldson & Preston, 1995; Egels-Zanden & Sandberg, 2010).

STAKEHOLDERS, THE SACRED & THE ETHICS OF CARE

Although the idea of stakeholder management is often seen as coming 'from a good place', the practice of systematically identifying stakeholders and their stakes and selecting strategies for engaging with them is often unpalatable for people. Crane & Ruebottom (2011) account for this dissatisfaction as it is based on rational economic principles from a managerial perspective. People may be identified by their firm as Muslims, women, African, LGBTQ stakeholders, etc., but these identities mean much more to them than the market segments that are projected onto them by an organisation. Crane & Ruebottom also highlight how this economisation of important social identities that appears to be continued to be espoused by instrumental approaches to stakeholder management often neglects disempowered minorities. In short, the practice of stakeholder identification can run the risk of isolating those who are most vulnerable from the stakeholder identification process. Economists refer to the practice of passing the cost of a transaction to individuals or groups who do not benefit from it as an 'externality' (Bakan, 2004). Individuals, groups and entities are frequently externalised by organisational and managerial processes to the extent that they become 'invisible' to decision-makers and consumers. Arlene Kaplan Daniels introduced the concept of *invisible work* in the late 1980s in a paper of the same name and it has since been used to characterise a range of work completed by people without economic reward and social recognition of the various costs to the invisible worker (Hatton, 2017). Lever & Milbourne (2017) demonstrated that strong immigration controls mean that some migrant workers have had to collude in making themselves more invisible in their work. Externalisation and invisibilisation are not intentional products of stakeholder identification processes, but they serve to highlight the importance of considering ways in which the concerns of the least powerful stakeholders are not lost, which may result greater exploitation.

Religion is a particularly useful field in which to discuss the roles and rights of stakeholders. William James's *The Varieties of Religious Experience* (1906) is now over 100 years old but remains an incredibly insightful analysis of how people experience religion in different ways throughout their lives. Although some people identify as deeply religious or spiritual and some feel completely irreligious, James writes that, for most people, religious experience is actually a spectrum that constantly changes throughout their life. James discusses a number of religious experiential phenomena but perhaps of most interest to the field of stakeholder analysis is the idea of the 'sacred'. Most people define the 'sacred' as that which is holy or worthy of respect. Treating something sacred disrespectfully is offensive to people who revere it. James, however, demonstrates that the idea of the sacred need not be solely understood as a religious construct. He points out that the best way to define the sacred is to think of it as something that a group feels must be treated with the utmost solemnity or *seriousness*. Treating something that people regard as sacred in a utilitarian, trivial or derisive way will produce strong reactions. Treating the sacred with anything less than the utmost seriousness and respectfulness makes the perpetrator appear profane. Whether you identify as deeply religious or completely atheistic, everyone holds certain ideas sacred. Scholars in the fields of critical management studies (Ackers & Preston, 1997; Bell & Taylor, 2004) and religious studies (Heelas, 1996; Carrette & King, 2005) have highlighted how a more spiritual discourse has become part of management training and organisational development since the 1990s. As religious and spiritual traditions and practice attempt to grapple with ethics at both a cosmological and social level, they offer a unique perspective on stakeholder theory that does not prioritise corporate or economic concerns over others (Wicks, 2014; Ray *et al*, 2014).

Businesses can risk violating principles when they attempt to commercialise or use ideas, practices, places or items that are held sacred in their product offerings or marketing strategies. Many people consider that the natural world, animals, childhood, family life, cultural traditions, aesthetics, etc. should be beyond the reach of the commercial realm. It is not just that these are considered sacred to stakeholders; many voices in stakeholder theory advocate that they be considered as stakeholders in their own right.

Mark Starik's paper, 'Should trees have managerial standing?' (1995), pointed out that the natural world is written out of much organisational and management theory. Despite this, human beings are not separate from nature; we are *part* of it and forgetting this is gradually leading us to self-destruct as a species. By considering stakeholders only to be humans with political-economic concerns, Starik draws attention to how stakeholder theory can treat nature as something that we human beings *use*, rather than something we *are*. Contributions from important theorists such as Starik have not only done much to push the development of the stakeholder concept beyond the realm of economic and human concerns, but also have led to a deeper consideration of who and what stakeholders actually are, and the degree of consideration they should be given by businesses and managers.

Carol Gilligan's *In a Different Voice* (1982) was instrumental to the development of the field known as the ethics of care. Rational ethical theory and stakeholder theory assume that stakeholders and decision-makers are conscious about the choices they are faced with making. This idea stems from moral developmental models that assume our ethical repertoire expands and becomes more sophisticated as we mature. Gilligan's research with women and girls found this not to be the case, and women were often 'dumbfounded' when asked to make an ethical decision. The moral development of girls is compromised through the lionisation of an ideal woman who selflessly facilitates social groups, family units and heterosexual relationships. The functioning of heteronormative organisations and patriarchal institutions depends on women remaining silent, and feeling guilt about raising their voice 'selfishly'. Whereas Kohlberg saw male ethical development as advancing towards an understanding of abstract principles, women's ethical development is conscious of relationships and connections. Males try to arrive at the 'right' answer to a moral dilemma, while females think of problems in terms of minimising damage to all in the relationship. While Gilligan's work was originally conceived as a feminist ethic of care, it has more recently been extended to non-human elements of organisational life (Connolly & Cullen, 2017). Organisational researchers have begun to examine the role of the animals as stakeholders in businesses. Animals are living beings who are worked, consumed and used without a consent that they are unable to give, and as such are excellent examples of silenced or invisible stakeholders. The ethics of care perspective has a huge potential to allow managers and organisations to connect to employees or stakeholders who are usually ignored in traditional identification practices.

7: Ethics as Corporate Practice: Corporate Social Responsibility, Citizenship & Governance

Many of the most influential thinkers on corporate social responsibility (CSR) define it as an evolving concept concerned with society's expectations of business – but what exactly is it? Many people assume CSR and business ethics are the same thing and both terms are often used to refer to sustainability initiatives, philanthropy, social entrepreneurship and corporate governance. With so many definitions of CSR, it is important to outline how it differs from related topics. This chapter discusses the first two business and society frameworks identified by Schwartz & Carroll (2008) – CSR and corporate citizenship – but it also examines important related concepts, such as corporate social performance and corporate governance.

More peer-reviewed research has been published on CSR than on any other business and society framework (Cullen, 2017) and it has become the central approach to studying the social and moral dimensions of moral life (Carroll, 2015).

Before considering what CSR is, we should reflect on *whether* it should exist. One of the most cited arguments against corporate social responsibility came from Milton Friedman in 1970, when he argued against it on economic, political and philosophical grounds. First, he wrote, if corporations are required to make social contributions, their profitability would be impacted and they would become less efficient. Second, Friedman claimed that it was undemocratic for corporations to use shareholders' funds to support 'good causes'. Finally, Friedman argued that corporations are not individuals and, because only individuals can have responsibilities, corporations do not have any.

Many supporters of CSR have responded to these positions by pointing out that Friedman believed in strategic altruism if businesses could use CSR for their own benefit. Governments that have embraced neo-liberal economic doctrines have granted organisations exceptional levels of freedom and licence. If organisations have received unprecedented rights and privileges, they must in turn honour their responsibilities to the people who have given these. Finally, many organisations have claimed the same rights as individuals.

CSR has changed alongside society's developing requirements of business. In the late 19th and early 20th centuries, the philanthropic activities of wealthy industrialists were the dominant mode by which industry 'gave back' to society. This changed radically in the 1960s, when the counter-culture began to demand greater levels of gender equality, civil rights and social and environmental engagement. Corporations' attempts to engage with these evolving norms radically altered the way in which CSR was done, effectively heralding much of the CSR activities that are recognisable today. CSR has since developed a level of acceptance within business communities that no other ethical framework enjoys to a similar extent.

Carroll (1999, 2015) claims that contemporary understanding of corporate social responsibility began in the 1950s and the key literature from this era understood what it was almost intuitively. Carroll reviewed how the concept of social responsibility had changed in the academic literature on the topic since that time. During the 1960s, there were attempts to formalise definitions of CSR by stipulating that businesses and managers had responsibilities that extended beyond their shareholders. During the 1970s, definitions and models of CSR began to proliferate and the idea that businesses should be *responsive* to the problems that their local communities and beyond were facing came to the fore. A key feature of many discussions of CSR in the 1970s was its voluntary nature; it was felt that businesses must not be legally held to act in a socially responsible way, but rather should voluntarily act in ways that did not necessarily profit them, but helped society and groups outside the business. Indeed, if CSR was a legal imposition on a firm that it had no choice to enact, it followed that the business could not have responsibility for its social initiatives.

Sethi (1975) clarified the term by distinguishing between an organisation's social *obligation*, social *responsibility* and social *responsiveness*. Social *obligation* is how an organisation responds to market forces in the economy and legal restrictions. Social *responsibility* goes beyond obligation to a stage where the organisation's norms and values align with society's expectations. The third stage is social *responsiveness*, where corporate behaviour proactively anticipates changing social norms and emerging problems, and changes how it does things to meet these.

In the 1970s, the first mentions of corporate social performance appeared. In 1979, Carroll developed a definition of businesses' social responsibility to encompass the economic, legal, ethical and discretionary expectations that society has for a business. In other words, society *expects* business to make a profit by producing the goods and services that it needs and wants, *but* to do so by meeting its expectations, helping groups and observing the law.

Carroll later proposed a pyramid of corporate social responsibility (1991), by which firms could assess the degree to which their CSR activities aligned with social requirements, expectations and desires. The foundational level of this pyramid is the level of *economic* responsibility. Firms are *required* to be profitable if they are to continue to exist, pay taxes and provide employment. The second level is the *legal* level, where firms are *required* to obey society's formal rules. The next level Carroll named the *ethical* level, where society *expects* firms to act in a way that is fair and does not harm stakeholders. The top and final level of Carroll's pyramid of CSR is the *philanthropic* level, where firms go beyond solely ethical responsibilities and actively contribute to the quality of life and act as a generous and responsible citizen in the larger community. This final level of CSR reflects the type of corporate activity that is *desired* by society.

It is important to observe that Carroll's levels of 'philanthropy' did not equate with more contemporary understandings of responsibility. Philanthropic responsibilities, in Carroll's model, involve being a good corporate citizen and engaging in activities that go beyond the expectations of society. Ethical responsibilities equate to abiding by the ethical norms of society. Legal responsibilities involve complying with and obeying the law. Economic responsibilities relate to the organisation's responsibilities to be profitable and to meet shareholders' expectations.

Carroll (with Schwartz, 2003) later revisited and revised this pyramid and depicted the key domains of the economic, legal and ethical responsibilities as interlocking circles in a Venn diagram. The intersections between these domains made it possible to suggest seven possible categories of CSR.

Schwartz & Carroll (2003) noted that few corporate activities were *purely ethical* in that they did not have economic or legal aspects. Perhaps one of the best-known examples of a corporate action that was purely ethical was Merck & Co's decision to make its treatment for river blindness (Ivermectin) freely available in less developed countries, and take no financial gain from it. Businesses that are *purely* concerned with operating *legally* may engage with unethical activities on the basis that there is no legal indictment for doing so. However, legal loopholes are often closed and companies that are solely concerned with remaining within the law despite ethical concerns about how they do things (such as 'head shops') soon find their grounds for operating declared illegal.

Companies that operate in the *purely economic* domain are concerned with generating profits at all costs and are unconcerned with ethical or legal principles unless these impact the organisation's cost-base. As legal concerns are marginal, they either skirt around the law or are minimally compliant with it.

At the intersection of the ethical domain with the economic domain, we find corporate initiatives based on the belief that solid social performance results in improved financial performance for organisations. Although the legal element is not as pronounced in this space, it is likely that organisations that adopt an economic/ethical perspective are likely to be legally compliant, at least in a passive way. This is the form of CSR that most people might be familiar with. On the other hand, at the nodal point of the ethical domain with the legal domain, we find organisations that meet their legal and ethical commitments because they want to, or have to. Reputational or economic gains that accrue to such organisations will be coincidental. This is not the same, however, as actively seeking compliance solely because of additional potential economic gains.

Corporate activities that combine the economic with the legal domain are often concerned with exploiting loopholes in legal systems to generate profits. Activities that focus on generating revenue within the law, while ignoring ethical concerns, include choosing to operate in countries or regions that do not have laws to uphold workers' rights or environmental protections.

Since the late 1950s, Ireland's economic policy has been to strategically attract and trade with large foreign-owned companies. Part of the strategy to attract foreign direct investment has been the reduction of Ireland's corporate tax rate to one of the lowest in the EU. Coupled with the fact that Ireland is an English-speaking, European country with a stable political and social climate, this creates advantages for Ireland. However, it has also meant that companies that have been supported in their development in their home countries can choose to strategically locate to Ireland and avoid paying higher rates of corporate tax in their home country. Nonetheless, many of the major companies Ireland has attracted often declare that it was not tax advantages alone that brought them. For example, many are attracted by Ireland's reputation for a hard-working, well-educated workforce, access to the European Union, and as an efficient location for intellectual property holdings. However, concerns have arisen in other jurisdictions about the extent of tax avoidance these companies have engaged in. Whereas tax minimisation or avoidance is not illegal, many have concerns about it as an ethically-suspect practice.

Finally, Schwartz & Carroll's (2003) model suggests that corporate activities that are simultaneously concerned with all three economic, legal and ethical domains are perhaps the space where most companies can be socially responsible. Such models of CSR are useful to us as scholars of the ethics of work and organisational life, but by thinking critically about such approaches we can find new ways to develop understandings of how CSR can be done.

At the outset of this section, it was mentioned that Schwartz & Carroll (2008) had identified corporate social responsibility to be one of the five main complementary networks by which businesses negotiate an ethical relationship with society. In their work, they suggest all five of these frameworks (which also include business ethics, stakeholder management, sustainability and corporate citizenship) share three core concepts: value, balance, and accountability. By *value*, they mean that businesses have opportunity to create net social value that produces the *outcome* of making the world better. By *balance*, they refer to the *process* of actively taking steps to meet the needs of diverse groups, rather than focusing on creating net social value for one group alone. By *accountability,* they are concerned with the *principles* of being responsible for actions and decisions taken, rather than treating groups or the natural world as an 'externality'.

CORPORATE SOCIAL RESPONSIBILITY & PERFORMANCE

In the 1980s, more emphasis was placed on the concept of corporate social performance than before. This was partly due to the need to operationalise it as a concept. This meant that organisations were keen to measure the effectiveness of their CSR activities but also to see how well these activities impacted on business performance. Corporate social performance is a means of assessing and transparently reporting on how well an organisation variously responds to important social concerns. This typically involves developing corporate social policies (formal statements or informal practices that reflect organisational values and principles) or social programmes (allocating corporate resources to activities that the company views as socially desirable) and measuring the social impacts of corporate behaviour on society. One such approach is triple bottom-line (3BL) accounting, where companies annually report on three key benchmarks: financial performance, social performance, and environmental performance.

Social performance is a hugely diverse area and organisations must select which elements they will focus on measuring to ensure that they do not betray their own mission and values. However, the measurement and recording of social impacts by business organisations has also provided researchers with an opportunity to answer questions about whether CSR not only works, but whether engaging in CSR can actually benefit firms.

There is still debate whether there is a solid relationship between corporate social performance (CSP) and corporate financial performance (CFP). One of the most cited studies was conducted by Orlitzsky *et al* in 2003 and involved a large scale meta-analysis of studies already conducted in this field. Interestingly, the researchers found a positive association between CSP and CFP across all studies and industries, which lead them to reconceptualise organisational effectiveness as a broad concept encompassing financial and social performance. Thus, firms are effective in the broadest sense, and this effectiveness is not just limited to solely social or financial performance. More recently, Margolis & Walsh (2003) reviewed 127 empirical studies on the relationship between social initiatives and firm financial performance and found there was a positive relationship in almost half of the results, with only seven studies pointing to a negative relationship, while 48 studies reported non-significant or mixed findings. On the basis of these findings, there is generally a positive relationship between the social performance and financial performance of businesses, but clearly much more research is needed. Carroll & Shabana (2010) have recently opened up this field of inquiry more by demonstrating that there is no single rationale for businesses becoming involved in 'doing' CSR, and that there are many outcomes and experiences that firms seek through being socially responsible.

Businesses that wish to be socially responsible often grapple with how to do so. Carroll's (1979) model of corporate social performance proposes that firms need to consider what social responsibility means for them and to identify the specific social issues they need to address and the ways in which they will respond to these issues as a corporation. The fact that this is presented as a conscious *choice*, however, might result in the social psychodynamics of organisational culture being ignored. For example, the process of vocational ideation (Cullen, 2013) discussed in **Chapter 3** requires individuals to consider whether they are oriented towards jobs (work that only rewards the individual at an economic level), careers (work that provides economic returns and self-advancement within a professional or organisational structure) or callings (work that the individual finds personally meaningful and is of service to others). Aguinis & Glavas (2013) demonstrate that organisations that are designed to facilitate meaningful, service-based work *embed* social responsibility into their structure, strategy and culture. The authors provide several examples of companies that achieve this; for example, a pet-supply company that established a foundation to find homes for orphaned animals. Companies that have *embedded* CSR not only find it is easier to achieve both their corporate and social goals, but also to attract employees who wish to engage in that mission also. Companies that have *peripheral CSR* (corporate CSR activities that are separate from the corporation's goals) tend to run less successful social responsibility initiatives.

Businesses that want to change their culture to one that is more socially and environmentally responsible, however, face a difficult task as most of the research on CSR tends be undertaken at the strategic and corporate level and the most important knowledge gaps in the field are at the level of individuals (Aguinis & Glavas, 2012). Although there are many stories about how individual firms changed and integrated CSR, there are few tools that organisations might adapt to assist them make this journey. One recent approach has been theorised by Maon *et al* (2010), based on changing each organisation's culture of engagement with its stakeholders. Maon *et al* use Jones *et al*'s (2007) typology of five stakeholder cultures to develop their approach. In this typology, one stakeholder culture is described as *amoral*, two have *limited morality* and two are *broadly moral*. The first stakeholder culture type is known as *agency* culture, which doesn't regard any stakeholders as relevant. As a result, the organisation is purely self-regarding and egotistic. The next stakeholder culture is known as the *corporate egotist* culture, which only regards shareholders as stakeholders, thus producing a short-term profit-maximisation orientation. The second *limited morality* culture is named as *instrumentalist,* where other stakeholders are recognised, but only on the basis of how they might be of instrumental utility to what shareholders want. The first *broadly moral* stakeholder culture type is *moralist,* which acknowledges all stakeholder interests and only sacrifices them in favour of financial gain when it is absolutely necessary to do so. The final stakeholder cultural type is the *altruist* culture, where concern for the welfare of stakeholders is the dominant and primary concern above all others.

Maon *et al* (2012) refer to Jones *et al*'s (2007) continuum of stakeholder culture types when outlining their model of the seven stages that organisations might engage with when embedding CSR as part of their development. These are divided into three cultural phases: the *cultural reluctance* phase is where the organisation resists the need to be socially responsible and retains an agency culture outlook (this phase includes the *dismissing stage*); the *cultural grasp phase* includes the stages when the organisation begins its CSR journey (this includes the *self-protecting,* the *compliance-seeking* and the *capability-seeking stages*); and the *cultural embedment* phase where the value of CSR to the organisation begins to become central to its cultural identity (and includes the *caring,* the *strategising* and the *transforming stages*).

At the *dismissing stage,* the organisation has no regard for stakeholders and has entirely contractual relationships with customers. This may create issues for the firm that can only be addressed by it engaging in CSR. As a result, it enters what is known as a *self-protecting* stage where CSR is engaged with in a peripheral way only, and only insofar as it protects the organisation. However, this draws managerial attention to the risks that are attached to not being CSR-active and so organisations develop policies and practices during a *compliance-seeking* stage that are aimed to lessen the organisation's liability and openness to reputational damage. The unintended result of these practices, however, is that an organisation's knowledge of the benefits of CSR increase during a *capability-seeking stage*. CSR now becomes more influential in the organisation. During the *caring* stage, relationships with stakeholders deepen further and the organisation becomes more socially proactive, with managers being given various CSR-related responsibilities. At the *strategising* stage, CSR becomes part of the espoused strategy of the organisation and the organisation seeks out opportunities to engage with social concerns. At the final stage, the *transforming stage*, the organisation integrates CSR principles into every aspect of organisational life.

CORPORATE CITIZENSHIP

The term 'corporate citizenship' (CC) is often used interchangeably with CSR, but it actually means something quite different and has the least amount of peer-reviewed published research on it (Cullen, 2017). Citizenship is the concept that defines the relationship between the individual and the state and is a two-way relationship based on rights and responsibilities. When applied to an organisation, it refers to the corporation's rights, duties and responsibilities in relation to the society in which it is a member (Carroll, 2015).

Matten & Crane (2005) proposed three different forms of CC – limited, equivalent and extended – that might be based on an organisation's ethical focus, its main stakeholders, its motivation or rationale for engaging in citizenship-based activities or the moral grounding on which it engaged with the concept. The *limited* view focuses on philanthropy and specific projects with an interest in giving something back to society. The *equivalent* view encompasses all areas of CSR and is motivated by the legal, economic and domains (as well as the philanthropic). Finally, the *extended* view is more concerned with the political realm and is driven by changes in the broader political milieu.

Matten & Crane (2005) point out that corporate citizenship is concerned with the various social, civil and political *rights* that organisations are increasingly being called on to deliver for citizens, particularly due to the contraction of government welfare and support programmes in countries that have embraced neo-liberalism.

Corporate Governance

Because business corporations have become significantly more politically significant, the area of corporate governance (CG) has become of critical concern to society. Carroll (2015) discussed how the social and economic impact of corporate ethical scandals in the early 2000s produced a new level of interest in CG and many believed that corporate legislation such as the US *Sarbanes-Oxley Act* (2002) would solve underlying governance problems. Failure to implement the act globally led to the stock market collapse in 2008 that, in turn, led to a deep, international recession.

Corporate governance (CG) is the name given to systems by which business corporations are directed and controlled. CG is usually theorised from an agency theory perspective (Jensen & Meckling, 1976), which proposes that the relationship between risk-bearer shareholders (or 'principals') and professional managers and executives (or 'agents') needs to be regulated in a way that ensures that agents do not exploit their access to information and resources for their own (rather than the principals') benefit.

There are two main types of CG approaches:

o The *framework* approach;

o The *regulatory* approach.

The *framework* approach is voluntarily led and provides a set of guidelines that require companies to abide by a set of operating standards or explain why they choose not to. The OECD has developed key principles of CG on this basis and has updated them over time to reflect changing norms in society and economic life. Different organisations may interpret or apply the principles of the framework in ways that are appropriate to their own organisation and sector as rules tend to be defined in the broadest possible way. This means that a greater level of flexibility is made available to the firm to handle changing circumstances or business environments. Ireland currently uses an approach to CG that could be described as *framework-led*.

The *regulatory* approach, on the other hand, requires firms to abide by a set of operating standards or face financial penalties. Although these rules may not be flexible enough to deal with new and changing circumstances or business environments, and may greatly limit the interpretation and application of rules, they also provide clear guidance on what *is* and what *is not* appropriate ethical and legal practice.

There are two important questions that the existence of the predominant CG approaches prompt:

o Do these forms of governance actually work in how they change the mindset and behaviours of individuals?

o Are there other ways of thinking about CG that transcend classifying it into rigid typologies of agents and principles or frameworks and regulation?

To answer the first question, we turn to the work of the French thinker Michel Foucault. Foucault's work has been hugely influential across all the social sciences and humanities and has addressed many social and ethical issues that have caused societies to re-consider how they treat people who have been considered 'abnormal' or 'deviant' in less understanding times. In a landmark work, *Discipline & Punish* (1975), Foucault demonstrates how criminal acts used to be punished in a way that was at first public (such as public execution or torture) or based on confinement (where the criminal was locked away from public view). Gradually, these punishments were replaced by techniques and processes that encouraged individuals to self-regulate their behaviour and thoughts. Foucault saw this change exemplified in Jeremy Bentham's 'Panopticon', an observational tower within a prison where wardens could potentially glance at any prisoner at any time, but the prisoners did not know when they were being observed. Not knowing this, they had to self-regulate their behaviour on the understanding that they were potentially under observation all the time. Enforcement is not required in a society where everyone self-polices. Anderson (2008), for example, has discussed how the London Stock Exchange introduced a non-binding 'Combined Code' following the financial scandals of the early 2000s, which resulted in questionable ethical practices that were not allowed in other financial jurisdictions. For CG to genuinely work, it needs to be supported by mechanisms that support self-discipline.

Aguilera & Jackson (2003) propose that CG involves relationships between three main stakeholder groups that influence important organisational practices such as deploying firm resources and making decisions. The first of these groups are the shareholders, whose interests depend on how liquid they are, how much equity (as opposed to debt) they carry and whether they invest capital to make more money, or for other non-financial reasons. The second group are employees, whose influence depends on national labour laws and the mobility of their skills and resources. The final group are managers, whose influence on CG depends on how much autonomy they have to make decisions and to control outcomes through financial or non-financial resources. Aguilera & Jackson demonstrate that there are many more influences on CG than solely the nature of the national regulatory environment.

A final response to Jensen & Meckling's (1976) conceptualisation of agency theory came from Davis *et al*'s (1997) *stewardship theory*. Taking issue with the economistic basic of agency theory, they proposed an approach to organisational theory that does not begin from an assumption that all parties are driven by self-interest. A *steward* is the opposite of an individualistic, amoral self-interested *agent*. *Stewards* demonstrate pro-organisational, collective behaviour and have greater utility for the principals than if they acted as an agent. Trusted stewards do not risk the organisation or anyone in it, and the costs associated with monitoring and regulating agents are removed. Stewards thus work best in organisations that allow them more power than if they acted as an agent. In short, stewards seek to benefit themselves by benefitting all. Stewardship emerges from a humanistic, psychologically-informed angle that runs counter to economic agency theory. The key challenge to enacting it is that risk-averse principals are unwilling to gamble with the level of trust that the steward requires. Principals worry that they might be agents in stewards' clothing! A potential solution to this difficulty might be found in the concept of *agonistic governance* (Fraher & Grint, 2016), which will be discussed in the final chapter of this book.

8: Ethics as Corporate Practice: Sustainability & Environmental Ethics

The protection and preservation of the natural world is the defining issue of the current era. Although global figures and institutions have stressed the critical nature of the looming climate crisis, it is perhaps more important that recognition for more sustainable ways of living, working and doing business has 'come from below'. The relationship between the natural world, economic sustainability and the just and fair treatment of all groups both at a local and global level is increasingly understood by all elements of society. There is a growing recognition that, if something does not change soon, weather systems will undergo such significant transformation that we will have to radically change our lives and societies. People who deny climate change are often decried as spokespeople for vested interests who would like to keep things as they are, despite a huge volume of scientific evidence and our day-to-day experiences of volatile weather conditions that point to the fact that the world is changing.

It is important to understand the forces that cause individuals and groups to choose to disregard the noticeably increased volatility of weather systems that are rapidly changing large sections of the planet and rendering them increasingly uninhabitable, as well as innumerable sources of scientific data. Cognitive dissonance (Festinger, 1957) may cause individuals to believe that there is conflict between their need for a sustainable income and living in a way that does not harm the natural world. To resolve this conflict, they choose the more immediate and short-term individual need and discredit the collective requirement for a sustainable biosphere. Social cognitive theory proposes that individuals *morally disengage* from their own behaviour that may harm others (Bandura, 2016) by: investing harmful practices with moral justifications; making it appear as if harmful practices actually help people; sanitising immoral behaviour in different language; downplaying, ignoring or misrepresenting the consequences of the action; dehumanising the victims of the action; blaming the victim for bringing it on themselves; placing the responsibility onto someone else; or diffusing it so it appears as if nobody is responsible.

Bandura and Festinger both theorise conscious responses to moral confusion. Psychoanalytic approaches also have much to offer our understanding of why some individuals choose to believe the vested interests that continue to try to convince an increasingly sceptical and concerned populace that climate change is not happening. Freud and his followers wrote extensively on the mechanisms by which the unconscious mind *defends* the ego from painful emotions such as anxiety and guilt. It is undoubtedly true that the enormity and pace of climate change is real and terrifying, so it is perhaps not surprising that our minds try to protect some people from believing it. One of the classic ego-defences is *repression*, where traumatic material is forced out of consciousness (but can still manifest in other forms). *Denial* involves the unconscious conspiring with the individual to block material that is just too upsetting or traumatic and convinces them that it is not happening (or has not happened). *Rationalisation* is another defence mechanism, whereby the individual distances themselves from their own experience of the trauma and views it in a way that they believe is disconnected.

Freud continued to return to ego-defence systems throughout his career and psychoanalytic researchers have discovered more since then. One of the most well-known of these forms of ego-defence is *identification with an aggressor*. When an individual is the subject of an unanticipated attack, they must deal with both the trauma of the verbal or physical assault *and* the shocking nature of it. If the victim tries to understand the assailant's perspective, they are engaging in *rationalisation.* If this develops to the stage where they agree and identify with the attacker, then they are experiencing what has become known as *Stockholm syndrome,* in which the victim defends themselves by becoming more like their attacker. Individuals who are surrounded by vociferous climate change deniers and conspiracy theorists, who may potentially control aspects of their occupational future, may feel that they have to compromise their personal beliefs in order to survive.

This broader social 'turn' to a concern for the natural environment is often discussed as an offshoot of the counter-culture movement of the 1960s. It is certainly the case that, from the 1970s onwards, there was a huge change in attitudes about the need to preserve the beauty and conserve the resources of the planet we share. This change in consciousness has been termed the 'new environmental paradigm' by Dunlap *et al* (2000). This paradigm (or worldview) was theorised as a nature-valuing alternative to the 'dominant social paradigm', which saw humanity as existing apart from nature, rather than as a component of it. As discussed in **Chapter 2** of this book, Eve Chiapello notes the emergence of a 'newer' spirit of capitalism that exists in concert with the natural world, rather than viewing it as a resource to be exploited. Adrian Parr (2009) has written how 'sustainability culture' increasingly places concern for the natural world at the centre of everything we use and consume, and issued a stark warning that we not be naive about 'greenwashed' products or services.

ETHICS & THE ENVIRONMENT

In a book on how moral philosophers have engaged with issues related to the environment, Patrick Curry (2011) points out that the three most influential and dominant schools of ethics (deontological approaches, consequentialism and virtue ethics) often fail to take nature into account. This, however, is probably due to the fact that man-made environmental degradation and pollution had not been a factor influencing life and commerce at a time when such traditions were founded. Any discussion of nature in relation to business involves considering whether we believe it holds an inherent value in itself, or whether we can view it as having an instrumental (or use) value. Inherent or intrinsic valuations of nature result in number of different environmental ethics value concepts such as:

o *Ecocentrism*, whose principal focus of value is on the natural world;

o *Zoocentrism*, whose principal focus of value is on animal life; or

o *Biocentrism*, whose principal focus of value is on all forms of life, both human and non-human (including animals and plants).

Anthropocentrism, on the other hand, has a principal focus of value on human beings. The anthropocentric perspective is most closely linked to *environmentalism*, which aims to persevere the bio-sphere *primarily* because doing so meets human interests.

It is often difficult to ascertain which environmental ethical position people hold. Curry (2011) classifies positions into three main fields – dark green, mid-green and light green ethics – varying according to the extent to which individuals are *anthropocentric* (the extent to which you consider *people* [humans] to be the central value that should be protected over all others) *versus eco-centric* (the extent to which you consider the *planet* [nature] to be the central value that should be protected over all others. When the perspective of *economism* (the extent to which one considers profit [free markets] to be the central value that should be protected over all others) is introduced, it is possible to construct a dual-axis matrix that organises the four main approaches to people, profit and planet to include an ethical position where concern for the natural world can coexist alongside an orientation towards responsible capitalism.

Imagine two axes: on the horizontal axis, we have a concern for people *versus* a concern for planet. On the vertical axis, we have a concern for people *versus* a concern for markets. If we place these together, we have the potential for four different positions.

If we are low on concern for profit, but high on concern for planet, we have a *dark green* ethical position. Dark green (or ecocentric) ethics holds that the integrity of species and ecosystems must be holistically defended. All elements should be treated equally and sometimes non-human elements must be allowed to win. White Jnr (1967) proposed that the emerging ecological crisis is rooted in Judeo-Christian religious thinking, which he believed privileged the next world over this world. This position is the opposite of a position known as *deep ecology* and deep green theory, which proposes that the divine can be found in, or is, the natural world.

If we are low on concern for planet and profit, but high on concern for people, we might have a *mid-green* ethical position. Mid-green theory (or intermediate environmental) ethics holds that value is not solely restricted to human beings and has a special interest in the ethics of how we work with and treat animals. From this perspective, an animal's inability to give consent for how they are treated means that we should accord them special moral status and protection. *Light green* theory (or environmentalism), which is represented by the ethical position of people who are high on belief of the importance of markets, but low on a sense of the relationship between people and nature, has been subjected to numerous critiques from ecological activists as it views nature as having slightly more *instrumental* than *intrinsic* value. It sees natural items as having an intrinsic value, but when they conflict with human interests, human needs take precedence.

This is not to say that these are the only environmental ethical positions available. Rather they are presented as a mechanism for reviewing the range of positions available to people. Other positions discussed by Curry include *eco-feminism*, which proposes that patriarchy's equating nature with 'the female' is used as an excuse to dominate both females and nature. Green virtue ethics extend the exhortation to find one's *telos* in life to finding our *telos* as humans in the biosphere. Finally, if one's ethical position values both markets and nature, it represents an attempt to reconcile the deepest regard for environment, people and profit, and is what has become known as corporate sustainability (Werbach, 2009).

Sustainability as a Corporate Practice

In 1990, Bassiry noted that the courses on social issues or ethics were often peripheral electives on MBA programmes, but by 2007 all the top 50 global MBA programmes included at least one course related to business, social or sustainability issues (Christiansen *et al*, 2007). The concept of 'sustainability' has grown massively important in business and management studies over this time period. Over the last 20 years, there has been a huge year-on-year increase of peer-reviewed articles published and cited on the topic of sustainability in the fields of business, management and organisational studies (Cullen, 2017). One need only search for conferences, seminars and training sessions on sustainability for managers to uncover the extent of the market for knowledge on all things sustainable amongst managers (Cotter & Cullen, 2012).

Sustainability is not a new concern, and there has been a substantial amount of activity in the field of development studies for some time. There has been something of an acceleration of interest in the area of sustainable business in the mainstream of management education in the aftermath of the global financial crisis when many populations over the world experienced the extent to which societies and economies had been subjected to unsustainable economic models.

Ask any person what they think 'sustainability' is about and they will usually respond that it is about protecting and preserving the natural environment. Sustainability, however, is much more than 'green' management. The most used definition sustainability appears to be that offered by Gro Harlem Brundtland (2010): 'meeting the needs of the present without compromising the ability of future generations to meet their own needs'. This means that sustainable development is concerned with delivering *and sustaining* returns across three dimensions: *people, planet* and *profit*. In the context of new or existing businesses, sustainability means that organisations should aim to produce *profits* in a sustainable way. This, in turn, means that they can sustain *people* by providing employment stability for local communities. The more profit that is made, the more consumers of the firm's goods, or users of its services, can benefit from price cuts or improved services.

Corporate sustainability also asks that firms proactively seek to repair the global ecosystem, even if they are not in a business that is usually associated with environmental pollution. The reason for this is that we are dependent on the natural world for our survival, and without it we cannot sustain ourselves as a species, let alone as a business! In *Strategy for Sustainability*, Adam Werbach (2009) asserts that organisations seeking to act sustainably should develop strategies based on the principles of sustainability, based on social, economic, environmental and cultural principles that must be executed concurrently.

Werbach posits these four components as 'co-equal' (in that organisations and managers who focus on only succeeding in one or two of these areas will ultimately fail in all), while others argue that aesthetic or psychological sustainability (or employees or consumers, etc.) should also be taken into account (Marshall & Toffel, 2005).

ENVIRONMENT & ORGANISATIONS

It is important to acknowledge the contribution of critical theorists who propose that capitalism and pro-environmental organisational behaviour are incompatible. Marx's analysis of industrial-era capitalism described a system where the owners of the means of production profit by not paying workers the true value of their labour, and claiming possession of irreplaceable resources that they then go on to mine and process. Traditional economics has demonstrated that societies based on consumption require constant cycles of production and consumption that generate huge amounts of waste. Economic growth has become the goal of many societies, despite the fact that GDP growth is often associated with high rates of pollution and environmental decay. This has led many critics to propose that ecological capitalism is not possible, and that corporate sustainability is a particularly insidious form of greenwashing.

In *The Ecology of Commerce,* Hawken (1993) writes that no company exists that has been created to intentionally harm society. This means that reform in the corporate sector that favours the environment is possible and should be driven from bottom-up approaches within the organisation. Rather than proposing that modernity and corporations are the sole source of all economic degradation, Hawken stresses that sustainable businesses can provide secure, stable, meaningful employment for people, which is needed for people to think in more sustainable ways.

Hart (1995) states that there are two types of environmental policy or strategy that a firm can adopt: *compliance* with legal and regulatory requirements; or a systematic *prevention* perspective that emphasises resource reduction and process innovation.

Russo & Fouts (1997) claim firms that tend towards the compliance approach differed in their resource base to those that tend toward prevention and have a greater ability to generate profits. This is because firms that choose the prevention approach focus on developing expertise in relation to resource reduction and process innovation. As a firm develops a focus on resource reduction, its processes and technologies become more sophisticated, which means it not only becomes expert at reducing waste and curtailing pollution, it also becomes a technological thought leader in its respective industry or sector. This in turn requires a more committed and sophisticated workforce, and better quality management. As the firm develops a reputation for being a leader in both its concern for the environment and in how it develops its technologies and processes, it will sell to a more socially and environmentally conscious market, attract talent to work for the organisation and develop strong levels of political acumen and capital. Socially responsible firms such as Interface, Patagonia and the Body Shop are high-profile examples of successful firms that not only live sustainable values, but also are profitable. The success of these firms is not only due to the emerging environmental ethic that is becoming critical to marketplaces, it is also directly related to the fact that the principles of sustainability have enabled them to remain profitable at no cost to the natural world. When genuine sustainability becomes the standard operating model in a given sector, it soon follows that sustainable goods and services will be expected by clients and consumers. In a world that is undergoing a strong and rapid turn to the sustainable, companies that genuinely embrace the principles of sustainability will garner a competitive advantage over those that do not.

As corporate sustainability is a new field, there are still many more questions that we need answered, which will be addressed by the managers and professionals of the future who are being educated in the new environmental and ecological paradigms of today. Towards the end of *The Protestant Ethic & The Spirit of Capitalism* (1992), Weber wrote that the Protestant work ethic was dependent on an industrial system that uses non-renewable resources. With these resources rapidly depleting, sustainable capitalism will require a new work ethic that will cause people to engage with preserving the natural world rather than fearfully denying or repressing our feelings about climate change. We need to understand how a pro-environment work ethic can be established in organisations and how the products and services of the present can change the way that work is done in the future. We need to understand how the relationship between acting sustainably can garner profits for organisations, and increase prosperity for all. Sustainability is very much a journey and it is easy for people to be cynical about the risk of greenwashing, particularly when mistakes are made along the way. However, it is important to bear in mind that working, managing and organising sustainably will very shortly no longer be a matter of choice if we are to preserve human life on earth.

9: International Business & Globalisation

From sole traders to large multinational enterprises (MNEs), all businesses transact at a global level. Although the small family shop you may have visited briefly this morning might appear to be a very local business, it actually lies at the intersection between many supply chains that span the planet. Because of this, addressing minor ethical dilemmas can provide solutions that impact positively at an entirely different point in the global supply chain. Failing to address these dilemmas, however, can result in problems arising. For example, a central problem in implementing a sustainability initiative in an organisation is that it attempts to provide a local solution to global problems. Individuals in one location are less likely to take the problems of other regions seriously if they feel that doing so will impact on their own interests. The problem with this selfish perspective is that it is ultimately self-defeating. People who are most affected by climate change, either through food scarcity or from the wars and conflicts that arise from these, are forced to migrate to less-affected areas. These areas, in turn, must absorb the cost of either controlling their borders, or of integrating new migrants within their society. If the threats to the natural biosphere are not taken seriously, chaos is a likely outcome. However, there is evidence that the need to develop a more integrated world that is respectful of nature is a growing *hypernorm,* which we discuss in the section on the ethics of International Business (IB) in this chapter. First, it is important to understand the *globalised* context in which IB occurs and the opportunities and ethical issues it brings to light.

GLOBALISATION

Globalisation is the process of national economic systems becoming more inter-reliant. As a term, 'globalisation' has only really entered common usage in the last 30 or so years. It is characterised by increasing interrelatedness and interconnectedness between national boundaries, corporate and governance structures. Globalisation accelerated in the 19th century with industrialisation, improved transportation and production technology, the development of the consumer culture and the creation of economic superpowers and MNEs. Modern economic globalisation began in earnest after World War II, when the international community sought to stabilise international relations in the world. The post-war Bretton Woods conference set up systems to regulate an international financial order (consisting of the World Bank, the International Monetary Fund and the short-lived International Trade Organisation). Economic globalisation was facilitated by cultural forms that enabled economic and political development, freed from geography. In turn, businesses restructured to be more 'networkable' (as opposed to hierarchical and bureaucratic) in the new global order. Since the 1980s, globalisation has grown at an exponential rate and unprecedented intensity. There is more than one reason for this growth (such as the Information Technology revolution, which has greatly enabled the capability of firms to conduct trade internationally), but perhaps the most significant driver over the last 40 years has been the advent of *neo-liberalism*.

There are many definitions of neo-liberalism, but in essence it is the belief that markets are the best and most rational mechanism for governing societies. It assumes that markets are the optimal way for governing societies and the fairest way of rewarding individuals. Although it does not deny that human beings are political, social, psychological, spiritual and political beings, it imagines that, above all, we are *economic* beings. Many economists have pointed out the fallacy of this belief, but neo-liberalism has become the dominant political and economic system in the world today (Harvey, 2005; Metcalf, 2017). Influenced by the work of economists such as John Maynard Keynes, who advocated that governments could manage economic growth through counter-cyclical activities, politicians such as Franklin D. Roosevelt addressed the social and economic devastation caused by the Great Depression by introducing programmes that sought to generate employment and curtail the excesses of the financial sector. Following the reconstruction programmes following World War II, concerns grew that the economic superpowers were losing competitiveness to the countries that had lost the mid-century conflict. By the early 1970s, commercial interests were worried that trade unions had grown too strong and social protections were too extensive to allow businesses in places such as the US and UK to be able to compete effectively against Japanese and German firms. Political leaders such as Margaret Thatcher and Ronald Reagan sought to 're-liberalise' the economies of their countries so that they could compete in the new post-war economic order. In practice, this meant that many industries that were traditionally supported by the state were privatised or closed down. As countries that put economic growth above all other social concerns increased their GDP, others were eventually forced to follow suit. Political parties that had been originally established to represent the rights of workers and the poor were forced to adopt pro-market policies. At a global level, under the influence of what has become a neo-liberal consensus, the market has become 'the only show in town'.

Any discussion of the ethics of globalisation should begin with a discussion of Immanuel Wallerstein's concept of the 'modern world system' (1974), which challenged the pre-1970s idea of first, second and third worlds based on their levels of capitalist enterprise, industrialisation and urbanisation. The classical solution to poverty and underdevelopment was to introduce more capitalism, industrialisation or urbanisation to encourage 'development'. Wallerstein challenged this by pointing out that the modern world system emerged from 16th and 17th century colonialism. European colonists exploited the resources of the countries they invaded and appropriated. Any capital accumulated as a result of these activities was sent back to the centre of various empires and thus further impoverished less 'developed' nations. Instead of thinking about first, second and third 'worlds', we need instead to think of one world with wealth and affluence at its core, a degree of interaction with this affluence and aspirations to join the centre at its semi-periphery, and powerlessness and poverty at the exploited periphery that continues to provide low-cost labour for the MNEs that typically reside at the core.

Is it fair to depict globalisation as an entirely negative process? Banerjee & Linstead (2001), for example, have said that the unity proposed by theorists who celebrate globalisation is actually a form of colonialism that is attempting to create a global culture of consumption. It might be truer to refer to it as 'the globalisation of capitalism'. For capitalism to work well, it requires stable social situations and an adult population who are free to work, earn and consume. Competition has resulted in technological innovations that allow people to communicate human rights abuses and have increased the quality and length of life in many locations. Because of the economic power of MNEs, they often have the potential to put pressure on national governments to address their ethical failures and create fairer societies. The reduction of trade barriers has also led to the growth of trade opportunities and increased employment.

The risks of 'borderless' financial activities were one of the main causes of the recent global financial crash. More recently, the reality of the way that certain borders are policed have forced people in vulnerable positions to take risks to cross borders and barriers, often with tragic consequences. Metcalf (2017) has pointed out that many of those who did not benefit from the promises of globalisation and neo-liberalism have turned towards proponents of popular nationalism who advocate building walls, strengthening borders and withdrawing from international trade mechanisms. In extreme cases, a globalised culture has been cited as the reason why some groups and parties reverted to notions of a national or racial identity. This is also the case with the rise of what some people have referred to as 'the new individualism', where people are more likely to plot out their own life trajectory rather than carrying on the traditions of whatever communities they have been born into. The prevalence of offshoring has led many to question how some of the richest corporations of the world use the global business environment to avoid paying taxes to the societies in which they operate.

Globalisation, however, is a fact of contemporary life. Many of the health, social, economic and environmental problems we face are global in nature. States, on their own, cannot solve these problems, which has led some to consider the benefits of global governance. Global problems cannot be solved on a national level, yet many of the international organisations established in the wake of World War II were designed to govern relationships between national bodies. As such they are not designed to actively solve global shared problems. The German sociologist, the late Ulrich Beck, wrote that Western democratic societies were entering a second modernity due to the globalising nature of modern institutions (1992). Everyday life in this globalising society has become 'de-traditionalised' and is breaking free from the traditions and customs of the past. Society used to be organised to facilitate the industrial order, but this industrial society is being replaced by a 'risk' society. Beck's 'risk society' concept theorises how globalisation creates new crises for people, institutions and the natural environment that have never been encountered before on earth. The solutions developed to manage and address these risks in turn create further unintended risks. The most significant risks to humanity emerge from our social development, as well as science and technology, and they impact on everyone and every part of our lives.

Global governance is not world government by a single institution or system; it is a movement towards integrating responses that impact on a global scale. Global governance is the evolving framework of rules, institutions and practices that set limits on the behaviour of individuals, organisations and companies. One of the areas in which global governance is clearly required relates to the issue of climate change. In November and December 2015, the COP21/CMP11 UN Climate Change Conference took place in Paris and attempted to establish a lasting, global agreement about measures that can be taken to save and protect the natural world. The agreement about concrete measures to reduce climate change will become binding when a threshold percentage of the largest atmospheric polluting companies sign up to the agreement, but in the interim, many countries have begun to apply their own legislative instruments to this process.

THE ETHICS OF INTERNATIONAL BUSINESS

Many business students take at least one course on International Business (IB) as an important part of their studies. IB is concerned with understanding the management and operation of firms in a globalised context. Because IB is concerned with global value chains, it often treats the ethical and moral issues that arise from jurisdictional differences and the social problems that result from doing business in a global marketplace. These include both legal issues (such as being asked for bribes by corrupt officials or intellectual property and copyright violations) and moral issues (such as worker exploitation in jurisdictions where employment or human rights laws are different or pollution of the natural world). Some management scholars have critiqued IB for disregarding its political context and contributing to the marginalisation of the vulnerable, impoverished and exploited populations (for example, Durepos *et al*, 2016). Others have demonstrated that, despite the growth of research in the fields of CSR and IB, *International CSR* is a hugely underdeveloped field (Pisani *et al*, 2017).

A number of agreements and mechanisms assist companies that conduct international trade – for example, national laws, *lex mercatoria*, the United Nations *Convention on Contracts for the International Sale of Goods*, or the UNIDROIT Principles.

It is important to realise that national law is not necessarily a unified concept and often emerges from sets of common law (a community's morality), civil law (the state's codified moral code, which it uses to govern its relationship with its citizens), customary law (community norms and morals) or civil law (faith traditions and religious customs). All of these are dynamic and not set in concrete, so they represent the conversations that various states have with themselves about their values. There are ethical dangers in this, though, as jurisdictions with laxer regulation are often chosen as the national legal setting for business covenants. MNEs, in particular, often tend to play off national systems against each other to ensure that they receive the best possible results for themselves.

Lex mercatoria refers to the custom and practice that traders developed in medieval times to regulate trading. These practices soon became augmented by official institutions and resulted in a form of *non-state* law that remains attractive to international business. A new version of international *lex mercatoria* is the UNIDROIT *Principles of International Commercial Contracts*, last revised in 2004. As it focuses on arbitration, it means that international disputes can be resolved in a less costly manner than other legal disputes and thus it is popular amongst businesses. Finally, the UN *Convention on Contracts for the International Sale of Goods*, which covers contract formation, performance and remedies in cases where contracts have been breached, was first passed in 1980 and has been ratified by 79 counties, including the most economically powerful in the world.

A useful tool for managers to help understand and address the ethical and moral issues that arise from doing business internationally is *integrated social contract theory* (Donaldson & Dunfee, 1999), which proposes that norms vary across the world. Some, however, are *hypernorms* – fundamental rights that are found in all cultures, religions and organisations and are acceptable to all. *Consistent* norms are specific to certain cultures or organisations, but are consistent with hypernorms and norms that are legitimate in other related cultures and economic systems. For example, countries that operate in societies where capitalism is the norm require all people to be treated equally based on their gender, sexual orientation, race, religion (or lack thereof). Norms and values that are more contentious within a cultural system are debated in a *moral free space. Illegitimate norms* are irreconcilable with hypernorms and they usually refer to practices that are considered immoral, such as prioritising profit over worker or customer safety.

From this perspective, CSR should help organisations focus their ethical practices to align with hypernorms (globally) and consistent norms (locally). On a more general level, CSR could ensure that an organisation's own consistent norms are not illegitimate and do not deviate from hypernorms. Integrated social contract theory (ISCT) demonstrates that managers working in an international context need to have a clear understanding of practical ethics theory in order to do their jobs. This is not a new idea and much research has been conducted to understanding the social and cultural differences between national cultures in order to help expatriate managers understand how to manage MNE subsidiaries or to close international trade deals. However, ISCT draws attention to the fact that managing the ethical differences that arise between cultures is often more of a craft than a science.

Said (1978) outlined the existence of a long-standing discourse known as 'orientalism', which presented a picture of 'non-Western' societies as irrational and unscientific. This biased discourse has been used to justify impose political and economic imperialism by certain countries over entire civilisations. 'Scientific' studies of cultural differences are often of limited utility to managers and professionals who work in transnational settings or with multicultural workforces. To begin with, they are conducted from the perspective of one culture, and attempt to shoehorn another country's cultural practices into a perspective that is alien to it. These studies are also often based on large-scale surveys that assume that all cultures are 'fixed', in that they do not change and all their members think about life and work in a singular fashion. Because of this, they tend to report broad tendencies and ignore diversity within groups or the personal psycho-history of individuals. Psychoanalysis seeks to understand the unconscious personal and cultural forces that influence an individual's life, but how can it be applied to the international business context?

If certain cultural facets are held sacred (for a definition of the sacred, see the section titled 'Stakeholders, the Sacred and the Ethics of Care' in **Chapter 6**), managers should of course be mindful of these when managing staff who may have different religious or cultural backgrounds. As managers may not be aware of their own cultural biases, psychoanalytic theory however is perhaps one of the best placed theories for helping managers understand themselves in international business contexts and multicultural workforces. One of Freud's earliest followers, Carl Jung, theorised a 'collective unconscious' that is shared by all humanity. This collective unconscious is the result of the evolution of our species' anxieties and desires over time. Jung saw evidence of this collective unconscious in various cultural groups' tendency to develop religious systems, myths, stories, archetypes and art that often were quite similar, regardless of the huge physical distances between these groups. For example, Jung (1984) writes that when we are unexpectedly struck by an artistic image in a deeply emotional way that surprises us, the image has resonated with us at the level of the collective unconscious. Because, according to Jung, we have inherited 'archetypes' (psychological blueprints for interpreting certain personalities), we are at risk of deploying these when we encounter individuals or groups who we do not necessarily understand.

In a famous essay on 'the uncanny', Freud (1919/2003) theorised that infantile complexes are the basis for belief systems (such as religions), fairy tales and myths. The *uncanny* is a feeling of dread, horror, repulsion or unpleasantness that suddenly arises when people encounter something familiar that is at the same time strange. Georg Simnel (1909) had earlier demonstrated how people who join a cultural group (usually for the purpose of business) from outside it (as opposed to being born into it) receive a special status of 'stranger'. This means that the person is considered a member of a cultural group, while at the same being seen as being distant from it. Freud discusses the use of the German word for the uncanny as the *unheimlich*, which translates as 'unhomelike'. Freud proposes our fear of the uncanny is actually the result of us repressing our fear of a place, thing, person, or the inevitability of death, etc. When something happens in our lives that causes the repressed experience to rise up again, we experience this released anxiety as dread. The uncanny arises from something that is, ironically, quite familiar to us that we have repressed. Being aware that encountering the culturally unfamiliar in our working lives can lead to apprehension can assist us to understand that the unknown and uncertain is an opportunity to learn about ourselves as managers. This is particularly the case when we manage or work with people from other cultural backgrounds.

10: Responsible Leadership

Leadership is a concept that has always garnered considerable attention in management and organisational theory. Given the huge impact that effective leadership has on the way that people think about their ethical roles and duties in society, it is important that we are conscious of the central role that leadership has in organisational settings. In a call for papers, Ciulla *et al* (2015) noted that, despite the huge volume of research that has been done on leadership, and the significant body of work on business ethics, the field of leadership ethics has received significantly less attention. This is curious, given that the ethical development and formation of leaders was one of the key topics in Plato's *Republic* (one of the foundational works of Western philosophy). In an earlier book (Cullen, 2008b), I discussed the way in which leadership theory has traditionally been described as following a path of development that first focused on studying a leader's *traits*, then their *behaviours*, before exploring the *situational* and *contingent* forces that influenced how leadership was done. In that book, I suggested that, around the turn of the millennium, dissatisfaction had begun to emerge in relation to the resurgence of *charismatic* leadership. Charismatic leadership is not a new idea: indeed, Max Weber identified *charisma* as being one of the three sources of authority or power within organisations. As mentioned earlier in this book, Weber established how religion was instrumental to the development of particular forms of capitalism. He also demonstrated how the religious concept of *charisma* (from the Greek word for 'grace' or 'gifted from God') could be bestowed on leaders by followers. The human tendency to associate outstanding performance as coming from a divine source often meant that individuals with exceptional leadership skills might be identified as having an 'outworldly' right and ability to lead.

Following a charismatic leader in charge might be inspiring, but it is not without dangers. In the 1980s, charismatic leadership underwent something of a resurgence and 'visionary' managers took over the running of companies, deploying high-energy forms of communication that entranced followers and the markets in turn. However, these performances often belied the character and ethics of such leaders: think of Leonardo DiCaprio's portrayal of Jordan Belfort in *The Wolf of Wall Street*!

In the early years of the new millennium, these neo-charismatic forms of leadership were often found to exist within organisations that were subsequently exposed as practicing creative accounting and poor corporate governance. Around that time, I noticed increased interest in what I then termed 'anti-charismatic' leadership theories, as they appeared to involve a counter-point to the bombastic style of charismatic leadership that had become prominent. I located the following three leadership theories in the 'anti-charismatic' space: *transformational* leadership; *servant* leadership; and *Level 5* leadership.

Anti-Charismatic Leadership

Transformational leadership as a concept was first discussed by James McGregor Burns in 1978 and was popularised in the field of business by influential theorists such as Bernard Bass. Transformational leadership remains one of the most influential and discussed theories of leadership, and research on it has grown each year since the mid-1980s (Cullen, 2015). Transformational leadership is quite a broad concept and research continues to extend its meaning and application. It can be summarised as being different to 'transactional leadership', where leaders reward followers (through bonuses, better work conditions, etc.) in return for improved performance or accepting changes. Transformational leadership, at least initially, partially focused on the values, beliefs and morals of followers and on how these could be transformed by, and with, the leader for the benefit of all. Later research and theory on transformational leadership emphasised elements other than the ethical, such as influencing, inspiring and stimulating followers (Delaney & Spoelstra, 2015). Because of this, transformational leadership has become something of an 'orthodoxy' within mainstream contemporary leadership studies but some theorists (for example, Tourish, 2013) have questioned the ethics of attempting to 'transform' the personal values of followers.

Another well-known group of approaches within ethical leadership is *servant leadership* (Greenleaf, 2002). Greenleaf advocated a form of leadership where the leader sees themselves at the service of those whom they follow. In this model, service is perceived as the primary motivation of the leader and is undertaken in complete service to others. Although Greenleaf proposed servant leadership as a philosophy rather than a prescriptive practice, Parris & Peachey (2013) found a diverse range of research projects and definitions of servant leadership.

In 2001, Jim Collins published the results of an independent research study of firms that had undergone a positive transformation and sustained their performance for over a decade in *Good to Great: Why Some Companies Make the Leap – and Others Don't. Good to Great* is fascinating because it explores a number of counterintuitive findings about corporate sustainability and change. One of the key concepts introduced, from a leadership perspective, is that of the *level 5 leader*. *Level 5 leaders* are individuals who temper an intense level of professionalism and personal resolve with a huge degree of humility. Focused on the development of the business that they have been charged to develop, they allow the credit for any successes to go to the individuals within the organisation who attained it, and any failures to themselves as leaders. Often, this commitment to their organisation is fostered through the years they worked within it before taking over as leader. In other words, they have a unique focus on what they must bring to the organisation and its people, rather than trying to do (or take) something to these for their personal benefit.

It would be an overstatement to claim that *transformational* (in the true sense), *servant*, or *level 5* leadership became popular as a reaction to the excesses of charismatic leadership, but it is noteworthy that they began to be discussed more in the aftermath of the corporate scandals of the early 2000s. The appeal of working for a leader who genuinely assumes their role to be one of ethical and moral support, who will not vilify failure or steal credit for work that they themselves have not done, perhaps goes without saying, but is there more to ethical leadership than merely being humble? In **Chapter 3**, we examined René Girard's concepts of *mimetic desire* and *mimetic rivalry*. Mimetic desire stems from a basic assumption that, besides our physical drives and instinctual desires, we do not really know what we want. Instead, we believe that we want certain things because we see other people desiring them. This leads us to see others who desire the same things as us as rivals. This is where conflict within groups arises from. Because desire is contagious, it puts groups, cultures and societies at risk. This risk can only be mitigated through the practice of *scapegoating*.

Scapegoating occurs when mimetic rivals transfer all the tensions arising in their conflict onto a singular individual or group. This scapegoat is isolated by the group, who behave violently towards him or her. When the scapegoat has been murdered or eliminated by the group, peace is restored and a new culture is established. Girard would later describe the sacrifice of Jesus, for example, as laying the foundation for Christian cultures, particularly as He was innocent of any crime. This form of leadership, where the leader sacrifices themselves in order to establish a new cultural or social group and to restore peace, is perhaps the most advanced form of anti-charismatic leadership.

Responsible Leadership & Context

Discussions of leadership from an ethical perspective tend to stress the strong moral character of the leader being studied. However, one person's leader is another person's enemy and it is always interesting to note the extent of counter-arguments to the supposed heroism of any given leader. In one of the most cited texts on leadership theory, Bennis (1989) states that the difference between management and leadership is that "managers do things right, while leaders do the right thing". This gives leadership a very clear moral remit ('doing the right thing'), but it also assumes that there is always one right thing to do. One of the deeper problems with a statement like this is that it assumes that leaders (who we usually think of as being the most senior people in an organisation or group) are people who have a better moral or ethical compass than the managers who work for them.

Keith Grint (2005) offered another model that differentiates managers from leaders. Instead of focusing on the personality of the leader or the situational contingency in which they find themselves, Grint focuses on the extent to which the problem faced is 'unstructured' (how poorly defined it is and how likely its solution will lead to more problems), and that a collaborative solution involving other parties will be required. If a problem is *critical* (such as an accident or an emergency), it will require very little collaboration, as the person in charge will need to take *command* of the situation. If the problem is clear and its cause has been established, it is considered *tame* and will require *management* to organise a process for to solve the problem. If the problem has never been encountered before, it is considered *wicked* and will require leaders to ask the right questions that will lead to a collaborative solution that none of the parties involved have ever met before. The lack of a clear success criteria for the implementation of a solution only makes wicked problems more difficult. This lack of clarity and structure is uncomfortable for many people, and perhaps demonstrates that, although most of mainstream leadership theory is concerned with celebrating the person of the leader, the experience of being a leader is not always pleasant for individuals who find themselves thrust into these positions. More importantly, it demonstrates that it is often very difficult to know what exactly is the right thing to do.

So how can we develop leaders in situations where problems are difficult to define and outcomes are uncertain? Fraher & Grint (2016) returned to this issue and pointed out that leaders are often exposed to critical, tame and wicked circumstances simultaneously and, as such, require a completely different mindset to dealing with each of them. This leadership mindset is named *agonistic governance* and is based on embracing uncertainty and complexity and treating *failure* as a key component of being a leader. This mindset is instilled in elite military units during their rigorous training and allows them to become familiar with ambivalence and failing in simulated environments. Imposing one leadership approach or a tried-and-tested management style on a confused or complicated problem often only results in short-term success. Fraher & Grint's paper 'Agonistic governance' (2016) challenges the idea that leaders should attempt to manage contexts in order to solve problems, and instead urges them to learn from them.

RESPONSIBLE FOLLOWERSHIP

Brown *et al* (2005) developed a model of ethical leadership that has become the dominant model in leadership and management studies (Ciulla *et al*, 2015). This model associates certain ethical leadership behaviours with positive outcomes for organisations, but questions remain as to its broader applicability outside the specific contexts in which it is applied. Although followers are mentioned in this model, they are somewhat less important than the leader.

Contemporary followership studies, on the other hand, focus on the extent to which followers create, construct or participate in the leadership of others. Collinson (2006), for example, suggested that there three main forms of follower identity. The first is *conformist* followers, who stereotypically follow their leaders. The next is *resistant* followers, who are the opposite of conformist followers and seek to resist and undermine those who have been placed in *headship* positions. *Headship* (Ladkin, 2015), is a formal position of authority that a person has been appointed to in an organisation, but it does not necessarily equate to the person being considered a leader or an authority (as many people who have been newly appointed to management or supervisory positions have found out!). *Dramaturgical* followers merely give leaders the impression that they are following them, whilst continuing to follow their own path. Clearly, resistant or dramaturgical followers do not engage in real followership activities, and so the rest of this section focuses on how followers construct, bestow and participate in leadership activities.

Critical and psychoanalytical approaches to followership focus on the extent to which the idea of leadership responds to a fundamental sense of 'lack' experienced by followers. The French psychiatrist and cultural theorist Jacques Lacan (2006) offered the idea that, once people become conscious of their own identity for the first time as children, they continually seek for a sense of completeness throughout their adult lives. This search for completeness means that people seek out leaders who will protect them from risk and an unstable sense of identity. Kelly (2014) has thus described leadership as an 'empty signifier' onto which people project their needs as followers.

Moral foundations theory (discussed in **Chapter 5**) has something to offer to this debate. Fehr *et al* (2015) asked how followers bestow a moral identity on leaders. Moral foundations theory distinguishes six discrete domains of human morality: care/harm; fairness/cheating; loyalty/betrayal; sanctity/degradation; authority/subversion; and liberty /oppression. Moralisation 'is the process through which an observer confers a leader's action with moral relevance' (2015: 184). Followers will *moralise* their leader's actions when these actions align with the followers' moral foundation, or with the foundation of the organisational culture. In other words, followers *project* an ethical perspective onto leaders when they see their own personal ethical foundations being modelled by him or her. This motivates followers to maintain moral self-regard for their moral reputation. These moral foundations, in turn, support different ethical leadership styles that generate motivations amongst followers to behave towards leaders in different ways.

This idea of *projection* has long been close to the core of psychoanalytic thinking. When the ego feels threatened by drives from the id or anxiety from the superego, it often defends itself by projecting threatening feelings onto another person or object. Frustrated with a lack of self-fulfilment, some groups even attempt to project their own experiences of inadequacy onto entire groups, cultures, religions or genders. This is a key component in the development of what Jean Lipman-Blumen has named 'toxic leadership' (2006). Toxic leaders poison entire organisations, societies and countries through destructive, disrespectful, corrupt or selfish practices. Interestingly though, the research on toxic leadership focuses on how and why followers allow them to behave the way they do and Lipman-Blumen proposes that this happens because of people's need to create and follow leaders. The reason why we need leaders (and why we'll accept toxic ones when ethical ones aren't available) is often due to us projecting our anxieties about our parents, mortality, etc. onto other people.

At a social level, social identity theory demonstrates how the groups we are members of, or aspire to be members of, can often impact on our self-concept. Different social contexts can trigger an individual to think, feel and act on the basis of their *social*, rather than their *individual*, selves. Strong levels of identification with groups that are more *salient* to the individual's identity can dominate an individual's cognitions and behaviours. Because some group affiliations and memberships are more salient to individuals than others, strong identification with one identity can enable unethical behaviours in other roles.

For example, if an individual's work identity is salient to them, they might use it to justify neglecting their family so they can prosper more in their organisation. Thus, an individual's social identity can justify being a moral employee over being an ethical parent. Social identity theory also has much to say about leadership in groups. Rather than choosing the best or most capable individual to lead them, groups tend to informally select leaders who are the most 'prototypical' of all members and their beliefs (Jackson & Parry, 2008). The leader in such groups serve the purpose of maintaining the cohesion of the group, rather than providing ethical or strategic direction, which can result in moral violations. Freud (1922) theorised that groups bonded together through libidinal ties or emotional attachments to leaders and other members.

The social identity perspective on groups of followers and their relationship with leaders is probably more observable in unstructured or informal groups (such as groups of friends or people with similar interests). Freud (1922) posited that this often accounted for followers regressing to child-like behaviour.

How does followership work in more formal workplace contexts where teams and groups are recruited, appointed and expected to deliver specific goals? One of the most enduring contributions made to analysing group psychodynamics was accomplished by Wilfred Bion of the Tavistock Institute. Following World War II, Bion worked with groups of demobilised soldiers and military personnel, but later diversified into working with work groups and teams. Bion (1961) recognised that there is another level to all work groups, which he named 'the basic assumption group'. This basic assumption was an underlying, unconscious belief or assumption about the real nature and purpose of the group. Bion categorised three basic assumptions. The first was the basic assumption of *dependency*. Groups based on this assumption were dependent on a leader in the group, who they believed had near magical powers to protect and sustain the group. Group members may eventually resent this feeling of powerlessness, or the leader may demonstrate that they are not as magical as the group believes, which results in a new leader being appointed. The second basic assumption was that of *flight/fight* mode. Groups based on this assumption are anxious that they may be subject to attack, which results in them appointing leaders who either embrace, or flee from, conflict. The final basic assumption is *pairing*. Any two members can resolve the group's problems, it is believed, by producing solutions (or fantasies) about better futures for the group. There have been many amendments and research projects conducted on Bion's theory of group dynamics, but perhaps most importantly, it demonstrates that groups of followers tend to develop unconscious systems for creating different conceptions of leadership that are open to dynamic change.

RETHINKING RESPONSIBILITY

There has been much interest in the concept of *responsible leadership* recently, but there is still little agreed definition, empirical research or theory in development. As a result, little is known about what it takes to be a responsible leader and the difficulties of being a responsible leader. Most research has been taken on organisational configurations of responsibility (CSR, sustainability, etc.), with little attention being paid to the leadership dimension of responsible management. Much ethical leadership theory has been criticised because it is conceptually vague, leader-centric and often highly contextual. More focus is needed on how to set ethical goals and on clarifying what the ethical outcomes of ethical leadership should be. Much responsible leadership theory does not have a distinct conceptual grounding. Voegtlin (2016) has attempted to provide this by referring to Iris Marion Young's extension of the concept of responsibility as a legal and political idea. Young (2006) challenged the legal concept of responsibility as one that attempted to establish blame for the consequences of certain actions. Instead, she proposed that responsibility for such consequences should be shared amongst people who could have indirectly solved such problems, particularly those who have the resources and power to remedy *structural* injustices. Structural injustice might be better thought of as the myriad ways in which institutions and social norms make it impossible for some individuals or groups to achieve what they want or need.

There are four dimensions of Young's model of proactive, extended responsibility. The first that it does not seek to *isolate* individuals for blame. This, in itself is a critique of direct liability, which seeks to isolate individuals responsible for something when it goes wrong. Young's model examines *background* conditions to assess whether they are unfair or unethical from the outset. It looks *forward*, as structural injustices cannot be changed by focusing on present concerns. Finally, it is shared and deployed through *collective action*, as all who contribute to social injustice (even indirectly) share responsibility for those harms. In other words, it recognises that, once we participate in a social system of any form (be it an organisation, a profession, a community or a society), we must consider ourselves *responsible* in a collective way when any element of it goes wrong. It is important to understand that being *responsible* is not the same as being *blameable* in Young's system. Blame is not a useful concept; its presence forces individuals to put energy into buffering themselves from the outcome of their decisions and actions. Ultimately, this does not help the resolution of these problems.

When applied to leadership, Young's model has a range of implications. Voegtlin (2016) proposes it to be a way of conceiving of responsible leadership as something simultaneously not isolated from broader social and environmental systems, critically aware of prevailing norms, and sharing responsibility for these problems with a view to participating in their collective resolution. Responsible leadership, when conceived this way, challenges the idea that leaders should be blamed or celebrated for their moral standing or business success, but might instead be thought of as individuals who seek to genuinely understand the *structure* of the situation in which they find themselves and to change it for the better of all.

Ethical responsible leadership, then, is a search for change that extends beyond the immediate *legal* responsibility of the individual leader. Like many forms of ethics in organisational life (such as sustainability and stakeholder theory), it involves looking outside the business to find new ways in which it can be improved by analysing ways in which life *outside* it can be improved. With so much moral risk attached to following and leading, and with so many of the processes by which we enact followership or project leadership repressed within our individual or group unconscious, how can we make sure that responsible leadership happens? Like so many psychoanalytic approaches, the key to doing this is by bringing unconscious processes into the light of our conscious thought.

One recent innovation in this area is the concept of the *implicit leadership theory* (ILT). Because there are more papers, books and theses written about leadership than any other topic in business and management studies (Cullen, 2008b), it follows that there are multiple definitions of leadership. In recent years, many people have been shocked that individuals who have displayed sexist, racist and elitist attitudes, limited intelligence and a lack of understanding of the position that they have sought have been elected to very powerful political roles. It is clear that leadership means different things to different people. ILTs are the unconsciously held beliefs that individuals have developed over their lifespan about what leadership is, and what it isn't. Because we are not aware of what them, ILTs are very powerful influencers of the type of follower or leader we will be (Cullen, 2015). In an excellent overview of implicit leadership theory, Alabdulhadi *et al* (2017) demonstrated that 40 years of research on ILTs has produced new concepts such as *implicit followership theories* (our tacitly held beliefs of what a good follower is), *implicit relationship theories* (our beliefs about whether quality work partnerships can develop over time) and *implicit voice theories* (followers' beliefs about whether it is appropriate to speak up to people in positions of authority). Because these are *implicit*, it means that we are not consciously of them. This lack of awareness has the potential to change us into a follower who supports immoral activities or a leader who violates their own ethical standards or social norms.

Like so many other theories discussed throughout this book, the way to protect ourselves and others from the guilt and anxiety associated with violating our ethical standards or harming others is to make unconscious beliefs and drives part of our conscious awareness, rather than unwittingly acting on them or being controlled by them. This is difficult, due to the manner in which our psyche represses them. Freud suggested a way through this through *free-association*: where the analyst mentions words or presents images to the analysand (the preferred term for the person undergoing psychoanalysis) in order to see what ideas, people, experiences they associate with them. To unearth your ILT, you might quickly answer the following questions: what is your definition of leadership?; who would you most like to be led by in your immediate working life?, and, who would you least like to be led by? Querying the reasons why you gave the answers may help you draft a personal ILT that will assist you recognise the form of leadership or followership that will lead you to prosper in your career and life.

FURTHER READING

The field of business ethics undergoes constant reappraisal and investigation. There is practically no area of business theory, working life or management practice that does not have some advanced work conducted on it. This knowledge is verified and communicated amongst scholars within peer-reviewed journals.

There are many rankings of journal quality, but the Association of Business Schools' *Academic Journal Guide* (2015) has become one of the most influential and most used in the UK, Ireland and beyond. The ABA rankings include a number of high quality ethics publications that are worth the perusal of budding business ethicists, as well as committed professionals and managers, including: *The Journal of Business Ethics*; *Business Ethics Quarterly*; *Business Ethics Review*; and *Business & Society*.

Many critical journals are often concerned with ethical issues; some of those that often publish interesting studies that apply critical theory or psychoanalytic approaches include: *Human Relations*; *Journal of Management Inquiry*; *Management Learning*; *Organisation Studies*; and *Organization*.

There are a number of excellent longer business, ethics and society textbooks available if readers wish to explore these areas in more detail. Manuel G. Velazquez's *Business Ethics: Concepts & Cases* is a very thorough, 'philosophically'-led exploration of the field. Crane & Matten's *Business Ethics: Managing Corporate Citizenship & Sustainability in the Age of Globalization* has just moved into its fourth edition and is one of the most comprehensive explorations of the field available. Andrew Wicks, Edward Freeman, Patricia Werhane and Kirsten Martin's *Business Ethics: A Managerial Approach* is also excellent. For an international perspective on business ethics, I recommend Janet Morrison's *Business Ethics: New Challenges in a Globalized World.*

The text that started the growth of stakeholder theory is R. Edward Freeman's *Strategic Management: A Stakeholder Perspective*, and I strongly recommend the articles by Laplume *et al* (2008) and Mitchell *et al* (1997) discussed in the text, which have made huge contributions to this field. Archie Carroll and Mark Schwartz's various writings on corporate social responsibility are cited and discussed in the text, and it goes without saying that they have had a huge influence in how I think about these areas and business ethics in general. I highly recommend engaging with the original writings of these important scholars cited in the reference section of this work.

In the field of sustainability and corporate environmental responsibility, Adam Werbach's *Strategy for Sustainability* has become something of a global best-seller in the field. Werbach's text is an excellent guide for managers implementing strategy, and he covers the fundamentals in an enthusiastic way.

It is important to remember voices that are critical of the ability of businesses to contribute to social and environmental sustainability also: Adrian Parr's *Hijacking Sustainability* in particular is highly recommended, and Patrick Curry's *Ecological Ethics: An Introduction* is essential reading for anybody concerned with protecting the natural world.

Many sociological texts are mentioned in the text and many try to inform how we think about work in the current era of capitalism. Karl Marx's *Capital*, Adam Smith's *The Wealth of Nations,* Karl Polanyi's *The Great Transformation* and Max Weber's *The Protestant Ethic & the Spirit of Capitalism* remain surprisingly relevant in the second decade of the third millennium. There is no doubt that the advent of neo-liberalism has entirely changed the world of work and organisations and so Francis Fukuyama's *The End of History & the Last Man* and David Harvey's *A Brief History of Neo-liberalism* are essential guides to understanding the forces that had led to the development of what some have called 'the new capitalism'. Just as interesting is the way in which these forces have produced 'new spirits' of capitalism. Luc Boltanski & Eve Chiapello's *New Spirit of Capitalism* has become something of a starting point for a whole new raft of research on the reasons for how and why people engage with this system. David Edgell's *The Sociology of Work: Continuity and Change in Paid and Unpaid Work* is a hugely readable introduction to the field of the sociology of employment and Guy Standing's *The Precariat: The New Dangerous Class* has provided some of the most important theoretical contributions on what the destabilisation of traditional working arrangements and roles has done to the *experience* of employment.

If I was asked to recommend one classic and one contemporary work on culture, I'd recommend Clifford Geertz's *The Interpretation of Cultures* and Tony Watson's *In Search of Management*. There are many excellent works on using psychoanalytic and psychodynamic work in organisations and I strongly recommend Yiannis Gabriel *et al*'s *Organisations in Depth* and Kenny *et al*'s *Understanding Identity & Organizations*.

Finally, leadership remains one of the key 'vessels' of ethics in organisational life. Given that more has been written and published about leadership than any other part of the business and management canon, it is difficult to narrow down books that succinctly capture the most important trends in leadership research and theory. Brad Jackson and Ken Parry's *A Very Short, Fairly Interesting and Reasonably Cheap Book About Studying Leadership* is everything it says in the title, and Brigid Carroll, Jackie Ford and Scott Taylor's *Leadership: Contemporary Critical Perspectives* offers a refreshing perspective on recent developments in the field.

REFERENCES

ACKERS, P. & PRESTON, D. (1997). Born again? The ethics and efficacy of the conversion experience in contemporary management development, *Journal of Management Studies*, 34, 677-701.

AGUILERA, R.V. & JACKSON, G. (2003). The cross-national diversity of corporate governance: Dimensions and determinants, *Academy of Management Review*, 28, 447-465.

AGUINIS, H. & GLAVAS, A. (2012). What we know and don't know about corporate social responsibility: A review and research agenda, *Journal of Management*, 38, 932-968.

AGUINIS, H. & GLAVAS, A. (2013). Embedded *versus* peripheral corporate social responsibility: Psychological foundations, *Industrial & Organizational Psychology – Perspectives on Science & Practice*, 6, 314-332.

ALABDULHADI, A., SCHYNS, B. & STAUDIGL, L.F. (2017). Implicit leadership theory *in* Curtis, E.A & Cullen, J.G. (eds.), *Leadership and Change for the Health Professional*, London: Open University Press.

ALLEN, T.E. (2014). 'Life of Pi and the moral wound', *Journal of the American Psychoanalytic Association*, 62, 965-982.

ALVESSON, M. (2002). *Understanding Organisational Culture*, London: Sage.

ANDERSON, G. (2008). *Cityboy: Beer and Loathing In The Square Mile*, London: Headline.

ANDERSON, R.C. (1999). *Mid-Course Correction: Towards a Sustainable Enterprise: The Interface Model*, Atlanta, GA: Peregrinzilla Press.

ANSCOMBE, E. (1958). Modern moral philosophy, available http://www.jstor.org/stable/3749051.

ARISTOTLE (1976). *The Ethics of Aristotle: The Nicomachean Ethics*, Harmondsworth, Penguin.

ARONSON, E. (2004). *The Social Animal*, New York: Worth.

BAKAN, J. (2004) *The Corporation: The Pathological Pursuit of Profit and Power*, London: Constable.

BANDURA, A. (2016). *Moral Disengagement: How People Do Harm And Live With Themselves*, New York: Worth Publishers/Macmillan Learning.

BANERJEE, S.B. & LINSTEAD, S.A. (2001). Globalization, multiculturalism and other fictions: Colonialism for the new millennium?, *Organization*, 8, 683.

BARENDS, E., TEN HAVE, S. & HULSMAN, F. (2012). Learning from other evidence-based practices: The case of medicine *in* ROUSSEAU, D. M. (ed.), *The Oxford Handbook of Evidence-Based Management*, Oxford: Oxford University Press.

BARRAQUIER, A. (2011). Ethical behaviour in practice: Decision outcomes and strategic implications, *British Journal of Management*, 22, S28-S46.

BASSIRY, G.R. (1990). Ethics, education and corporate leadership, *Journal of Business Ethics*, 9, 799-805.

BAUMAN, Z. (1998). *Work, consumerism and the new poor,* Buckingham, PA: Open University Press.

BAUMAN, Z. (2011). *The London riots – On consumerism coming home to roost* [online], Social Europe, available http://www.socialeurope.eu/2011/08/the-london-riots-on-consumerism-coming-home-to-roost/ [accessed 5 February 2015].

BECK, U. (1992). *Risk Society: Towards a New Modernity*, London: Sage.

BECKER, E. (2011). *The Denial of Death,* London: Souvenir.

BELL, D. (1974). *The Coming of Post-industrial Society,* London: Heinemann Education.

BELL, E. & TAYLOR, S. (2004). 'From outward bound to inward bound': The prophetic voices and discursive practices of spiritual management development, *Human Relations*, 57, 439-466.

BELL, E., TAYLOR, S. & DRISCOLL, C. (2012). Varieties of organizational soul: The ethics of belief in organizations, *Organization*, 19, 425-439.

BENNIS, W. (1989). *On Becoming a Leader,* New York: Perseus Books.

BERGMAN, J.Z., WESTERMAN, J.W. & DALY, J.P. (2010). Narcissism in management education, *Academy of Management Learning & Education*, 9, 119-131.

Berman, S.L. & Johnson-Cramer. M.E. (2016). Stakeholder theory: Seeing the field through the forest, *Business & Society*, 13, 95-121.

BION, W.R. (1961). *Experiences in Groups, and Other Papers*, London: Tavistock Publications.

BLAUNER, R. (1964). *Alienation and Freedom: The Factory Worker and His Industry,* Chicago: University of Chicago Press.

BOLTANSKI, L. & CHIAPELLO, E. (2005). *The New Spirit of Capitalism,* London: Verso.

BOLTANSKI, L. & THÉVENOT, L. (2006). *On Justification: Economies of Worth*, Princeton/Oxford, Princeton University Press.

BOURDIEU, P. (1990). *In Other Words: Essays towards a Reflexive Sociology*, Stanford, CA: Stanford University Press.

BRAVERMAN, H. (1974). *Labour and Monopoly Capital: The Degradation of Work in the Twentieth Century*, New York: Monthly Review Press.

BROWN, M.E., TREVINO, L.K. & HARRISON, D.A. (2005). Ethical leadership: A social learning perspective for construct development and testing, *Organizational Behavior & Human Decision Processes*, 97, 117-134.

BROWNING, C.R.A. (2001). *Ordinary Men: Reserve Police Battalion 101 & the Final Solution in Poland*, revised edition, Harmondsworth: Penguin.

BRUNDTLAND, G.H. (2010). Foreword, *in* SMITH, M.H., HARGROVES, K. & DESHA, C. (eds.), *Cents and Sustainability: Securing Our Common Future by Decoupling Economic Growth from Environmental Pressures*, New York: Routledge.

BURKEMAN, O. (2016). Therapy wars: The revenge of Freud, *The Guardian*, 7 January, available: www.theguardian.com/science/2016/han/07/therapy-wars-revenge-of-freud-cognitive-behavioural-therapy [accessed 7 June 2016].

CARRETTE, J.R. & KING, R. (2005). *Selling Spirituality: The Silent Takeover of Religion*, London/New York: Routledge.

CARROLL, A.B. (1979). A three-dimensional conceptual model of corporate performance, *Academy of Management Review*, 4, 497-505.

CARROLL, A.B. (1991). The pyramid of corporate social responsibility: Toward the moral management of organizational stakeholders, *Business Horizons*, 34, 39-48.

CARROLL, A.B. (1999). Corporate social responsibility: Evolution of a definitional construct, *Business & Society*, 38, 268-295.

CARROLL, A.B. (2015). Corporate social responsibility: The centerpiece of competing and complementary frameworks, *Organizational Dynamics*, 44, 87-96.

CARROLL, A.B. & SHABANA, K.M. (2010). The business case for corporate social responsibility: A review of concepts, research and practice, *International Journal of Management Reviews*, 12, 85-105.

CARROLL, B., FORD, J. & TAYLOR, S. (2015). *Leadership: Contemporary Critical Perspectives*, London: Sage.

CASEY, C. (1999). 'Come, join our family': Discipline and integration in corporate organizational culture', *Human Relations*, 52, 155-178.

CAYLEY, D. (2001). *The Scapegoat: The Ideas of René Girard, Part 1*, Ottawa: Canadian Broadcasting Corporation (Radio).

CHARTERED ASSOCIATION OF BUSINESS SCHOOLS (2015). *Academic Journal Guide,* London: Chartered Association of Business Schools.

CHIAPELLO, E. (2013). Capitalism and its criticisms, *in* GAY, P.D. & MORGAN, G. (eds.), *New Spirits of Capitalism?: Crises, Justifications and Dynamics,* Oxford: Oxford University Press.

CHRISTIANSEN, L.J., PIERCE, E., HARTMAN, L.P., HOFFMAN, W.M. & CARRIER, J. (2007). Ethics, CSR, and sustainability education in the *Financial Times* top 50 global business schools: Baseline data and future research directions, *Journal of Business Ethics,* 73, 347-368.

CIULLA, J.B., KNIGHTS, D., MABEY, C. & TOMKINS, L. (2015). Call for Papers: Special Issue on Philosophical Approaches to Leadership Ethics, *Business Ethics Quarterly,* available http://journals.cambridge.org/images/fileUpload/documents/BEQ_Call_for_Papers_-_2016.pdf.

COLLINS, J.C. (2001). *Good to Great: Why Some Companies Make the Leap – and Others Don't,* London: Random House Business.

COLLINSON, D. (2006). Rethinking followership: A post-structuralist analysis of follower identities, *The Leadership Quarterly,* 17, 179-189.

CONNOLLY, L. & CULLEN, J.G. (2017). Animals and organisations: An ethic of care framework, *Organization & Environment,* 1-19.

COTTER, R.J. & CULLEN, J.G. (2012). Reflexive management learning: An integrative review and a conceptual typology, *Human Resource Development Review,* 11, 227-253.

CRAFT, J. (2013). A review of the empirical ethical decision-making literature: 2004-2011, *Journal of Business Ethics,* 117, 221-259.

CRANE, A. & MATTEN, D. (2016). *Business Ethics: Managing Corporate Citizenship & Sustainability in the Age of Globalisation,* 4e, Oxford: Oxford University Press.

CRANE, A. & RUEBOTTOM, T. (2011). Stakeholder theory and social identity: Rethinking stakeholder identification, *Journal of Business Ethics,* 102, 77-87.

CRONENBERG, D. (2012). Director's commentary, *A Dangerous Method.*

CULIBERG, B. & MIHELIC, K.K. (2016). The evolution of whistleblowing studies: A critical review and research agenda, *Journal of Business Ethics,* 1-17.

CULLEN, J. (2008a). Self, soul and management learning: Constructing the genre of the spiritualised manager, *Journal of Management, Spirituality & Religion,* 5, 264-292.

CULLEN, J. (2008b). *Communication and Knowledge Sharing at Work,* Dublin: Blackhall Publishing.

CULLEN, J.G. (2004). Identifying sectoral management cultures through recruitment advertising, *Leadership & Organization Development Journal*, 25, 279-291.

CULLEN, J.G. (2009). How to sell your soul and still get into Heaven: Steven Covey's epiphany-inducing technology of effective selfhood, *Human Relations*, 62, 1231-1254.

CULLEN, J.G. (2011a). Differentiating between vocations and careers, *in* COLLECTION, M.U.E. (ed.), Maynooth: Maynooth University.

CULLEN, J.G. (2011b). Researching workplace spiritualisation through auto/ethnography, *Journal of Management, Spirituality & Religion*, 8, 143-164.

CULLEN, J.G. (2013). Vocational ideation and management career development, *Journal of Management Development*, 32, 932-944.

CULLEN, J.G. (2015). Leading through contingencies *in* CARROLL, B., FORD, J. & SCOTT TAYLOR, J.F. (ed.), *Leadership: Contemporary Critical Perspectives*, London: Sage: 45-68.

CULLEN, J.G. (2017). Educating business students about sustainability: A bibliometric review of current trends and research needs, *Journal of Business Ethics,* 145.429-439.

CUNLIFFE, A.L. (2004). On becoming a critically reflexive practitioner, *Journal of Management Education*, 28, 407-426.

CURRIE, G., KNIGHTS, D. & STARKEY, K. (2010). Introduction: A post-crisis critical reflection on business schools, *British Journal of Management*, 21, s1-s5.

CURRY, P. (2011). *Ecological Ethics: An Introduction,* Cambridge: Polity Press.

DANIELS, A.K. (1987). Invisible work, *Social Problems*, 34, 403-415.

DAVIS, J.H., SCHOORMAN, F.D. & DONALDSON, L. (1997). Toward a stewardship theory of management, *Academy of Management Review*, 22, 20-47.

DE MONTAIGNE, M. (2003). *The Complete Essays*, London: Penguin.

DEAL, T.E. & KENNEDY, A.A. (1982). *Corporate Culture: The Rites and Rituals of Corporate Life*, Wokingham, Addison-Wesley Publishing Company Inc.

DELANEY, H. & SPOELSTRA, S. (2015). Transformational leadership: Secularized theology? *in* CARROLL, B., FORD, J. & SCOTT TAYLOR, J.F. (ed.), *Leadership: Contemporary Critical Perspectives*, London: Sage.

DESAI, S.D. & KOUCHAKI, M. (2017). Moral symbols: A necklace of garlic against unethical requests, *Academy of Management Journal*, 60, 7-28.

DIXON, N.F. (1976). *On the Psychology of Military Incompetence*, London: Cape.

DONALDSON, T. & DUNFEE, T.W. (1999). When ethics travel: The promise and peril of global business ethics, *California Management Review*, 41, 45-63.

DONALDSON, T. & PRESTON, L.E. (1995). The stakeholder theory of the corporation: Concepts, evidence, and implications, *Academy of Management Review*, 20, 65-91.

DUNLAP, R.E., VAN LIERE, K.D. & MERTIG, A.G. (2000). Measuring endorsement of the New Ecological Paradigm: A revised NEP scale, *Journal of Social Issues,* 56, 425.

DUREPOS, G., PRASAD, A. & VILLANUEVA, C.E. (2016). How might we study international business to account for marginalized subjects?, *Critical Perspectives on International Business*, 12, 306-314.

DUTA, A., SETLIFF, T. & BOGER, C. (2011). Mind matters: A neurofeedback business ethics case study, *Journal of Business Ethics Education*, 8, 255-264.

EDGELL, S. (2006). *The Sociology of Work: Continuity and Change in Paid and Unpaid Work*, London: Sage.

EGELS-ZANDEN, N. & SANDBERG, J. (2010). Distinctions in descriptive and instrumental stakeholder theory: A challenge for empirical research, *Business Ethics – A European Review*, 19, 35-49.

Elias, N. (1978). *The Civilizing Process: Vol.I, The History of Manners*, New York: Pantheon Books.

ELIAS, N. (1982). *The Civilizing Process: Vol.II, State Formation and Civilization*, Oxford: Blackwell.

ETZIONI, A. (1964). *Modern Organizations*, Englewood Cliffs, NJ: Prentice-Hall.

FARAH, M.J. (2012). Neuroethics: The ethical, legal, and societal impact of neuroscience, *Annual Review of Psychology*, 63, 571-591.

FAYOL, H. (1949). *General and Industrial Management*, translated by STORR, C., London: Pitman.

FEHR, R., KAI CHI, Y.A.M. & DANG, C. (2015). Moralized leadership: The construction and consequences of leader perceptions, *Academy of Management Review*, 40, 182-209.

FESTINGER, L. (1957). *A Theory of Cognitive Dissonance*, Stanford, CA: Stanford University Press.

FLORES, J., BARUCA, A. & SALDIVAR, R. (2014). Is neuromarketing ethical? Consumers say "Yes". Consumers say "No", *Journal of Legal, Ethical & Regulatory Issues*, 17, 77-91.

FORSYTH, D.R. (1980). A taxonomy of ethical ideologies, *Journal of Personality and Social Psychology,* 39, 175-184.

FOUCAULT, M. (1975, trans. 1977). *Discipline and Punish: The Birth of the Prison*, Harmondsworth: Penguin.

FRAHER, A. & GRINT, K. (2016). Agonistic governance: The antinomies of decision-making in U.S. Navy SEALs, *Leadership*, 1-20.

FRANCIS, Pope (2015). *Laudato Si': On Care of Our Common Home*, Encyclical Letter, available http://w2.vatican.va/content/francesco/en/encyclicals/documents/papa-francesco_20150524_enciclica-laudato-si.html [Accessed 28 July 2015].

FREEMAN, R.E. (2010). *Strategic Management: A Stakeholder Approach*, Cambridge: Cambridge University Press.

FREUD, S. (1922). *Group Psychology and the Analysis of the Ego*, London: The International Psycho-Analytical Press.

FREUD, S. (1974). *Introductory Lectures on Psychoanalysis*, Harmondsworth: Penguin.

FREUD, S. (2001). *The Future of an Illusion: Civilisation & its Discontents and Other Works*, London: Penguin.

FREUD, S. (2003). *The Uncanny*, New York: Penguin.

FRIEDMAN, M. (1970). The social responsibility of business is to increase its profits, *New York Times Magazine*, 13 September.

FUKUYAMA, F. (1992). *The End of History and the Last Man*, New York: Free Press.

GABRIEL, Y. (1999). *Organizations in Depth: The Psychoanalysis of Organizations*, London: Sage.

GABRIEL, Y. & CARR, A. (2002). Organizations, management and psychoanalysis: An overview, *Journal of Managerial Psychology*, 17, 348.

GABRIEL, Y., HIRSCHHORN, L., MCCOLLOM HAMPTON, M., SCHWARTS, H.S. & SWOGGER JR, G. (1999). *Organizations in Depth: The Psychoanalysis of Organizations*, London: SAGE.

GEERTZ, C. (1973). *The Interpretation of Cultures*, New York: Basic Books.

GHOSHAL, S. (2005). Bad management theories are destroying good management practices, *Academy of Management Learning & Education*, 4, 75-91.

GIDDENS, A. (1992). Introduction, in GIDDENS, A., *The Protestant Ethic and the Spirit of Capitalism*, London: Routledge.

GIDDENS, A. & SUTTON, P.W. (2013). *Sociology*, Cambridge: Polity Press.

GILLIGAN, C. (1982). *In a Different Voice: Psychological Theory and Women's Development*, Cambridge, MA: Harvard University Press.

GIRARD, R. (1966). *Deceit, Desire, and the Novel: Self and Other in Literary Structure*, Baltimore, MD: Johns Hopkins Press.

GOTTFREDSON, L.S. (1981). Circumscription and compromise: A developmental theory of occupational aspirations, *Journal of Counseling Psychology*, 28, 545-579.

GREENLEAF, R.K. (2002). *Servant Leadership: A Journey into the Nature of Legitimate Power and Greatness*, New York: Paulist Press.

GRINT, K. (2005). Problems, problems, problems: The social construction of 'leadership', *Human Relations*, 58, 1467-1494.

HAIDT, J. (2012). *The Righteous Mind: Why Good People are Divided by Politics and Religion*, New York: Pantheon.

HAKIM, C. (2011). *Honey Money: The Power of Erotic Capital*, London: Allen Lane.

HALL, C.S. (1954). *A Primer of Freudian Psychology*, Cleveland, OH: World Publishing Co.

HALL, P.A. & SOSKICE, D.W. (2001). *Varieties of Capitalism: The Institutional Foundations of Comparative Advantage*, Oxford, Oxford University Press.

HANDY, C. (1993). *Understanding Organisations*, 4e, Harmondsworth: Penguin.

HART, S.L. (1995). A natural resource-based view of the firm, *Academy of Management Review*, 20, 986-1014.

HARVEY, D. (2005). *A Brief History of Neo-liberalism*, Oxford: Oxford University Press.

HATTON, E. (2017). Mechanisms of invisibility: Rethinking the concept of invisible work, *Work Employment & Society*, 31, 336-351.

HATZFELD, J. (2005). *A Time for Machetes: The Rwandan Genocide: The Killers Speak: A Report*, London: Serpent's Tail.

HAWKEN, P. (1993). *The Ecology of Commerce: A Declaration of Sustainability*, New York: HarperCollins.

HAYEK, F.A.V. (1944). *The Road to Serfdom*, London: Routledge.

HEELAS, P. (1996). *The New Age Movement: The Celebration of the Self and the Sacralization of Modernity*, Cambridge, MA: Blackwell.

HEELAS, P. (2008). *Spiritualities of Life: New Age Romanticism and Consumptive Capitalism*, Malden, MA: Blackwell.

HEELAS, P. & WOODHEAD, L. (2005). *The Spiritual Revolution: Why Religion is Giving Way to Spirituality*, Oxford: Blackwell.

HEYES, A. (2005). The economics of vocation or 'why is a badly paid nurse a good nurse'?, *Journal of Health Economics*, 24, 561-569.

HO, K.Z. (2009). *Liquidated: An Ethnography of Wall Street*, Durham, NC: Duke University Press.

HOCHSCHILD, A.R. (1983). *The Managed Heart: Commercialization of Human Feeling*, Berkeley, CA: University of California Press.

HOCHSCHILD, A.R. (2003). *The Commercialization of Intimate Life: Notes from Home and Work*, Berkeley, CA: University of California Press.

HOFSTEDE, G.H. (2001). *Culture's Consequences: Comparing Values, Behaviors, Institutions and Organizations across Nations*, 2e, Thousand Oaks, CA: Sage Publications.

HUPPATZ, K. (2012). *Gender Capital at Work: Intersections of Femininity, Masculinity, Class and Occupation*, Basingstoke: Palgrave Macmillan.

HUPPATZ, K. & GOODWIN, S. (2013). Masculinised jobs, feminised jobs and men's 'gender capital' experiences: Understanding occupational segregation in Australia, *Journal of Sociology*, 49, 291-308.

HUPPATZ, K.E. (2010). Class and career choice: Motivations, aspirations, identity and mobility for women in paid caring work, *Journal of Sociology*, 46, 118-132.

HYDE, P. & THOMAS, A.B. (2002). Organisational defences revisited: Systems and contexts, *Journal of Managerial Psychology*, 17, 408.

INGHAM, G.K. (2008). *Capitalism*, Cambridge: Polity.

JACKSON, B. & PARRY, K. (2008). *A Very Short, Fairly Interesting and Reasonably Cheap Book about Studying Leadership*, London: Sage.

JAMES, K. & CLARK, G. (2002). Service organisations: Issues in transition and anxiety containment, *Journal of Managerial Psychology*, 17, 394-407.

JAMES, W. (1906). *The Varieties of Religious Experience: A Study in Human Nature*, London: Longman.

JANKO, R. (1987). Introduction *in* JANKO, R. (trans.), *Poetics 1*, Indianapolis: Hackett Publishing Company, ix-xxvi.

JENSEN, M.C. & MECKLING, W.H. (1976). Theory of a firm: Managerial behaviour, agency costs and ownership structure, *Journal of Financial Economics*, 3, 305-360.

JOHNSON, G. (1992). Managing strategic change: Strategy, culture and action, *Long Range Planning*, 25, 28-36.

JOHNSON, G., SCHOLES, K. & WHITTINGTON, R. (2005). *Exploring Corporate Strategy: Text and Cases*, Harlow: Financial Times Prentice Hall.

JONES, T.M. (1991). Ethical decision-making by individuals in organizations: An issue-contingent model, *Academy of Management Review*, 16, 366-395.

JONES, T.M., FELPS, W. & BIGLEY, G.A. (2007). Ethical theory and stakeholder related decisions: The role of stakeholder culture, *Academy of Management Review*, 32, 137–155.

JUNG, C.G. (1984). *The Spirit In Man, Art & Literature*, London: Ark.

KELLY, S. (2014). Towards a negative ontology of leadership, *Human Relations*, 67, 905-922.

KENNY, K., WHITTLE, A. & WILMOTT, H. (2011). *Understanding Identity & Organisations*, London: Sage.

KLEIN, N. (2008). *The Shock Doctrine: The Rise of Disaster Capitalism*, London: Penguin.

KLUCKHOHN, F. & STRODTBECK, F.L. (1973). *Variations in Value Orientations*, Westport, CT: Greenwood Press.

KOLB, D.A. (1984). *Experiential Learning: Learning as the Source of Learning and Development*, Upper Saddle River, NJ: Prentice-Hall.

KRISTEVA, J. (2012). A tragedy and a dream: Disability revisited, The Michael Devlin lecture, *The Wounded Body: Human Vulnerability and Disability in a Finite World* seminar, 29 September, Maynooth: Saint Patrick's College.

KROEBER, A.L. & KLUCKHOHN, C. (1952). *Culture: A Critical Review of Concepts and Definitions*, Cambridge, MA: The Museum.

LACAN, J. (2006). The mirror stage as formative of the I function as revealed in psychoanalytic experience, *Ecrits*, New York: W.W. Norton: 93-81.

LADKIN, D. (2015). Leadership, management and headship: Power, emotion and authority in organizations *in* CARROLL, B., FORD, J. & SCOTT TAYLOR, J.F. (eds.), *Leadership: Contemporary Critical Perspectives*, London: Sage: 3-25.

LAING, R.D. (1990). *The Divided Self: An Existential Study in Sanity & Madness*, Harmondsworth: Penguin.

LAND, C. & TAYLOR, S. (2010). Surf's up: Work, life, balance and brand in a New Age capitalist organization, *Sociology*, 44, 395-413.

LAND, C. & TAYLOR, S. (2014). The good old days yet to come: Postalgic times for the new spirit of capitalism, *Management & Organizational History*, 9, 202-219.

LAPLUME, A.O., SONPAR, K. & LITZ, R.A. (2008). Stakeholder theory: Reviewing a theory that moves us, *Journal of Management*, 34, 1152-1189.

LAVÉ, J. & WENGER, E. (1991). *Situated Learning: Legitimate Peripheral Participation*, Cambridge: Cambridge University Press.

LEVER, J. & MILBOURNE, P. (2017). The structural invisibility of outsiders: The role of migrant labour in the meat-processing industry, *Sociology*, 51, 306-322.

LIPMAN-BLUMEN, J. (2006). *The Allure of Toxic Leaders: Why We Follow Destructive Bosses and Corrupt Politicians – and How We Can Survive Them*, Oxford: Oxford University Press.

LITZ, B.T., STEIN, N., DELANEY, E., LEBOWITZ, L., NASH, W.P., SILVA, C. & MAGUEN, S. (2009). Moral injury and moral repair in war veterans: A preliminary model and intervention strategy, *Clinical Psychology Review*, 29, 695-706.

LOCKE, J. (1772). *Two Treatises of Government*, London: J. Whiston, W. Strahan, J. and F. Rivington, L. Davis, W. Owen and others.

MACINTYRE, A. (1979). Seven traits for the future, *The Hastings Center Report*, 9, 5-7.

MAON, F., LINDGREEN, A. & SWAEN, V. (2010). Organizational stages and cultural phases: A critical review and a consolidative model of corporate social responsibility development, *International Journal of Management Reviews*, 12, 20-38.

MARGOLIS, J.D. & WALSH, J.P. (2003). Misery loves companies: Rethinking social initiatives by business, *Administrative Science Quarterly*, 48, 268-305.

MARQUARDT, N. & HOEGER, R. (2009.) The effect of implicit moral attitudes on managerial decision-making: An implicit social cognition approach, *Journal of Business Ethics*, 85, 157-171.

MARSHALL, J.D. & TOFFEL, M.W. (2005). Framing the elusive concept of sustainability: A sustainability hierarchy, *Environmental Science & Technology*, 39, 673-682.

MARTIN, J. (1992). *Cultures in Organizations: Three Perspectives*, New York: Oxford University Press.

MARTIN, R. (2002). *Financialization of Daily Life*, Philadelphia: Temple University Press.

MARX, K. (1995). *Capital: An Abridged Edition*, Oxford: Oxford University Press.

MARX, K. & ENGELS, F. (2004). *The Communist Manifesto*, London: Penguin.

MASON, P. (2015). *Postcapitalism: A Guide to Our Future*, New York: Farrar, Straus & Giroux.

MATTEN, D. & CRANE, A. (2005). Corporate citizenship: Toward an extended theoretical conceptualization, *Academy of Management Review*, 30, 166-179.

MENZIES, I. (1960). A case-study in the functioning of social systems as a defence against anxiety, *Human Relations*, 13, 95-121.

METCALF, S. (2017). Neo-liberalism: The idea that swallowed the world, *The Guardian* [online], available: doi: [accessed 20 October 2017].

MIGIRO, K. (2014). The killer: "I was like an animal", Thomson Reuters Foundation News, available: http://news.trust.org//item/20140402103837-orbum/ [accessed 15 June 2017].

MILES, R.E. & SNOW, C.C. (1978). *Organizational Strategy, Structure, and Process*, London: McGraw-Hill Education.

MILGRAM, S. (1974). *Obedience to Authority: An Experimental View*, London: Pinter & Martin.

MINTZBERG, H. (1975). The manager's job: Folklore and fact, *Harvard Business Review*, 53, 49-61.

MINTZBERG, H. (2004). *Managers not MBAs: A Hard Look at the Soft Practice of Managing and Management Development*, New Jersey: Pearson Education.

MITCHELL, R.K., AGLE, B.R. & WOOD, D.J. (1997). Toward a stakeholder theory of stakeholder identification and salience: Defining the principle of who and what really counts, *Academy of Management Review*, 22, 853-886.

MONBIOT, G. (2016). Neo-liberalism – the ideology at the root of all our problems, *The Guardian*, available: https://www.theguardian.com/books/2016/apr/15/neoliberalism-ideology-problem-george-monbiot [accessed 7 November 2017].

MORGAN, G. (1986). *Images of Organization*, London: Sage.

MORRISON, J. (2015). *Business Ethics: New Challenges in a Globalized World*, New York: Palgrave.

MOXNES, P. (2017). Anxiety and organization: What I learned about anxiety in a psychiatric ward in the 70s that turned out to be useful for managers in daily practice, *Culture & Organization*, Forthcoming, 1-14.

O'FALLON, M.J. & BUTTERFIELD, K.D. (2005). A review of the empirical ethical decision-making literature: 1996-2003, *Journal of Business Ethics*, 59, 375-413.

OBAMA, B. (2013). Inaugural address, Washington DC: Office of the Press Secretary, The White House.

OECD (2015). *G20/OECD Principles of Corporate Governance: OECD Report to G20 Finance Ministers and Central Bank Governors*, Paris: Organisation for Economic Co-operation and Development.

ORLITZKY, M., SCHMIDT, F.L. & RYNES, S.L. (2003). Corporate social and financial performance: A meta-analysis, *Organization Studies*, 24, 403-441.

OSNOS, E. (2011). Meet Dr. Freud, *The New Yorker,* 10 January 10, 54-63.

PARKER, M. (2000) *Organizational Culture and Identity: Unity and Division at Work*, Thousand Oaks, CA: Sage.

PARKER, M. (2001). Stuck in GUM: Life in a clap clinic, *in* HIRSCH, D.N. & HIRSCH, E. (eds.), *Inside Organizations: Anthropologists at Work*, Oxford: Bloomsbury Academic.

PARKER, M. (2004). Becoming manager, or the werewolf looks anxiously in a mirror, checking for unusual facial hair, *Management Learning*, 35, 45-59.

PARR, A. (2009). *Hijacking Sustainability*, Cambridge, MA: MIT.

PARRIS, D. & PEACHEY, J. (2013). A systematic literature review of servant leadership theory in organizational contexts, *Journal of Business Ethics*, 113, 377-393.

PETERS, T.J. & WATERMAN, R.H. (1984). *In Search Of Excellence: Lessons From America's Best-Run Companies*, New York: Warner Books.

PHILLIPS, M. (2013). On being green and being enterprising: Narrative and the ecopreneurial self, *Organization*, 20, 794-817.

PISANI, N., KOURULA, A., KOLK, A. & MEIJER, R. (2017). How global is international CSR research? Insights and recommendations from a systematic review, *Journal of World Business*, 52, 591-614.

PLATO (1985). *The Republic*, 1st ed., translated by STERLING, R.W. & SCOTT, W.C., New York: Norton.

POLANYI, K. (1957). *The Great Transformation: The Political and Economic Origins of Our Time*, Boston, MA: Beacon Press.

RAWLS, J. (1971). *A Theory of Justice*, Cambridge, MA: Harvard University Press.

RAY, D.E., BERMAN, S.L., JOHNSON-CRAMER, M.E. & VAN BUREN III, H.J. (2014). Refining normative stakeholder theory: Insights from Judaism, Christianity, and Islam, *Journal of Management, Spirituality & Religion* 11, 331-356.

REED, D.R.C. (1997). *Following Kohlberg: Liberalism and the Practice of Democratic Community*, Notre Dame, IN: University of Notre Dame Press.

REST, J.R. (1986). *Moral Development: Advances in Research and Theory*, New York: Praeger.

REYNOLDS, S.J., LEAVITT, K. & DECELLES, K.A. (2010). Automatic ethics: The effects of implicit assumptions and contextual cues on moral behavior, *Journal of Applied Psychology*, 95, 752-760.

RITZER, G. (1996). *Modern Sociological Theory*, London: McGraw-Hill.

ROKEACH, M. (1973). *The Nature of Human Values*, New York: Free Press.

ROSE, N. & ABI-RACHED, J. (2013). *Neuro: The New Brain Sciences & the Management of the Mind*, Oxford: Oxford University Press.

RUSSO, M.V. & FOUTS, P.A. (1997). A resource-based perspective on corporate environmental performance and profitability, *Academy of Management Journal*, 40, 534-559.

SAID, E. (1978). *Orientalism*, New York: Pantheon.

SCHEIN, E. (1996). Three cultures of management: The key to organisational learning, *Sloan Management Review*, 38, 9-20.

SCHEPER-HUGHES, N. (1979). *Saints, Scholars and Schizophrenics: Mental Illness in Rural Ireland*, Berkeley, CA: University of California Press.

SCHEPER-HUGHES, N. (1992). *Death without Weeping: The Violence of Everyday Life in Brazil*, Berkeley, CA: University of California Press.

SCHWARTZ, M.S. (2006). God as a managerial stakeholder? *Journal of Business Ethics*, 66, 291-306.

SCHWARTZ, M.S. & CARROLL, A.B. (2003). Corporate social responsibility: A three-domain approach, *Business Ethics Quarterly*, 13, 503-530.

SCHWARTZ, M.S. & CARROLL, A.B. (2008). Integrating and unifying competing and complementary frameworks: The search for a common core in the business and society field, *Business & Society*, 47, 148-186.

SETHI, S.P. (1975). Dimensions of corporate social performance: An analytical framework, *California Management Review*, 17, 58-64.

SHAY, J. (1994). *Achilles in Vietnam: Combat Trauma and the Undoing of Character*, New York: Atheneum/Oxford: Maxwell Macmillan International.

SHAY, J. (2002). *Odysseus in America: Combat Trauma and the Trials of Homecoming*, New York: Scribner.

SHEDLER, J. (2010). The efficacy of psychodynamic psychotherapy, *American Psychologist*, 65, 98-109.

SHTEYNBERG, G. (2015). Shared attention at the origin: On the psychological power of descriptive norms, *Journal of Cross-Cultural Psychology*, 46, 1245-1251.

SHWEDER, R.A. (1991). *Thinking Through Cultures: Expeditions In Cultural Psychology*, Cambridge, MA: Harvard University Press.

SMIRCICH, L. (1983). Concepts of culture and organizational analysis, *Administrative Science Quarterly*, 28, 339-358.

SMITH, A. (1970). *The Wealth of Nations*, Harmondsworth: Penguin.

STANDING, G. (2011). *The Precariat: The New Dangerous Class*, London: Bloomsbury Academic.

STARIK, M. (1995). Should trees have managerial standing? Toward stakeholder status for non-human nature, *Journal of Business Ethics*, 14, 207-217.

TAYLOR, F.W. (1911). *The Principles of Scientific Management*, New York: Harper & Brothers.

TOURISH, D. (2013). *The Dark Side of Transformational Leadership: A Critical Perspective*, New York: Routledge.

TROMPENAARS, A. & HAMPDEN-TURNER, C. (2012). *Riding The Waves of Culture: Understanding Diversity in Global Business*, 3e, London: Nicholas Brealey.

UNIDROIT (2004). *Principles of International Commercial Contracts*, Rome: International Institute of the Unification of Private Law.

UNITED NATIONS (1948). *Universal Declaration of Human Rights*, New York: United Nations.

UNITED NATIONS (2010). *Convention on Contracts for the International Sale of Goods*, New York: United Nations.

VAUGHAN, D. (1996). *The Challenger Launch Decision: Risky Technology, Culture and Deviance at NASA,* Chicago: University of Chicago Press.

VELASQUEZ, M. (2011). *Business Ethics: Concepts & Cases*, 7e, New York: Pearson.

VOEGTLIN, C. (2016). What does it mean to be responsible? Addressing the missing responsibility dimension in ethical leadership research, *Leadership*, 12, 581-608.

VYGOTSKY, L. S. (1978). *Mind in Society: The Development of Higher Psychological Processes*, translated by COLE, M., JOHN-STEINER, V., SCRIBNER, S. & SOUBERMAN, E., Cambridge, MA: Harvard University Press.

WALLACE, C. (2009). Your company on the couch, *Financial Times*, Business Life, 12 November, 1.

WALLERSTEIN, I.M. (1974). *The Modern World-system*, New York: Academic Press.

WATSON, T.J. (2001). *In Search of Management: Culture, Chaos and Control in Managerial Work*, London: Thomson Learning.

WEBER, M. (1919). *Science as Vocation*, available at http://tems.umn.edu/pdf/WeberScienceVocation.pdf. [Accessed 22 July 2011].

WEBER, M. (1992). *The Protestant Ethic and the Spirit of Capitalism,* London/New York: Routledge.

WERBACH, A. (2009). *Strategy for Sustainability: A Business Manifesto,* Boston, MA: Harvard Business School Press.

WHITE JNR, L. (1967). The historical roots of our ecologic crisis, *Science,* 155, 1203-1207.

WHYTE, W.H. (1961). *The Organization Man*, Harmondsworth: Penguin.

WICKS, A. (2014). Stakeholder theory & spirituality', *Journal of Management, Spirituality & Religion*, 11, 294-306.

WICKS, A., FREEMAN, E., WERHANE, P. & Martin, K. (2009). *Business Ethics: A Managerial Approach*, New York: Pearson.

WILLIAMS, R. (1988). *Keywords: A Vocabulary of Culture and Society*, revised and expanded ed., London: Fontana Press.

WRIGHT, C., NYBERG, D. & GRANT, D. (2012). 'Hippies on the third floor': Climate change, narrative identity and the micro-politics of corporate environmentalism, *Organization Studies*, 35, 1451-1475.

YOUNG, I.M. (2006). Responsibility and global justice: A social connection
    model, *Social Philosophy & Policy*, 23: 102-130.
ZIMBARDO, P.G. (2007). *The Lucifer Effect: Understanding How Good
    People Turn Evil*, New York: Random House.
ZIMMERMAN, E. & RACINE, E. (2012). Ethical issues in the translation of
    social neuroscience: A policy analysis of current guidelines for public
    dialogue in human research, *Accountability in Research: Policies &
    Quality Assurance*, 19, 27-46.
ZITTOUN, T. & GILLESPIE, A. (2015). Internalization: How culture
    becomes mind', *Culture & Psychology*, 21, 477-491.
ZIZEK, S. (2011). *Living in the End Times*, London/New York: Verso.
ZOHAR, D. & MARSHALL, I.N. (2005). *Spiritual Capital: Wealth We Can
    Live By*, San Francisco: Berrett-Kohler.

ABOUT THE AUTHOR

Before becoming an academic, John G. Cullen worked, managed and consulted for a variety of organisations in the private, not-for-profit and public sectors. Prior to joining Maynooth University School of Business John taught and researched at the Irish Management Institute and Dublin Institute of Technology. At Maynooth, he teaches courses on business ethics and society, organisational behaviour, management and leadership.

John's research explores how ethics, values and beliefs influence the ways people work and manage in contemporary organisations and society. He is particularly interested in how the sustainability discourse influences responsible management education and work ethics. His peer-reviewed research work has been published in highly-ranked journals such as *Human Relations, the Journal of Business Ethics, Work, Employment & Society, Organization & Environment, Culture & Organization* and the *Journal of Information Science*.

OAK TREE PRESS

Oak Tree Press develops and delivers information, advice and resources for entrepreneurs and managers. It is Ireland's leading business book publisher, with an unrivalled reputation for quality titles across business, management, HR, law, marketing and enterprise topics. NuBooks is its ebooks-only imprint, publishing short, focused ebooks for busy entrepreneurs and managers.

In addition, Oak Tree Press occupies a unique position in start-up and small business support in Ireland through its standard-setting titles, as well training courses, mentoring and advisory services.

Oak Tree Press is comfortable across a range of communication media – print, web and training, focusing always on the effective communication of business information.

OAK TREE PRESS
E: info@oaktreepress.com
W: www.oaktreepress.com / www.SuccessStore.com.